MW01296147

A Grow Your Own Way Publication:

Heirloom style produce for fun and profit:

A marketing guidebook for 25 heirloom vegetables for market gardeners, urban growers, small farms, or homesteads.

By: Jason McClure

Jason McClure is a farm visionary, entrepreneur, and writer. He grew up on a cattle farm with his grandparents. Jason grew up on a farm in his family since the 1800s. Jason's primary farm mentor was his grandfather, born in 1900. Jim, his grandfather, used many practices that would be classified today as sustainable and organic practices.

After leaving the family farm after his grandfather's death, Jason earned a business degree, MBA, Master's in Communication, and a graduate certificate in Applied Statistics. He has spent time in corporate America and has returned to his roots in the Ozarks Mountains in North Central Arkansas. Here he and his wife, Sarah, and two sons, Calvin and Graham, are building Ozark Family Farm.

Other books by Jason

BIG IDEAS,
SMALL FARM

A marketing guide for attracting customers, increasing profitability, and building community

Jason McClure

Author of *Heirloom Style Produce for Fun and Profit*

A Grow Your Own Way Publication

Jason McClure

SMALL

Grow Yourself

FARM

Grow People, Products, and Profits

LEADERSHIP

A Grow Your Own Way Book

TABLE OF CONTENTS

Guiding Philosophy

Here is what I believe. I believe that opportunity is alive and well in rural America. I believe that people can still make a living off the land. I believe that farm life is the best life. I believe there is no place I would rather be than on my rocky hill on the Salem Plateau of the Ozark Mountains. I believe that there is nothing better than reflecting on that day's achievements while sitting on my porch in the evening. I believe that a bad day farming is still better than the best day in a cubicle. I believe my grandfather was right when he said, *"rest is better when you earn it."*

My name is Jason McClure; my wife and I own Ozark Family Farm in Moko, Ar. We started this adventure in 2015 with the purchase of 100 acres of land. We sell our produce, pork, chicken, and beef directly to our friends, and we invite our friends to visit our farm and stay in one of our rustic cabins or sleep in a barn.

The purpose of this book is to share what I have learned during this process. I hope you will gain some insights into what works and what doesn't work. During this process, I have made mistakes, and I have learned much. I am glad to share that with you.

Today, people are looking for farm-fresh products. The demand is vast, but the supply is limited. The more producers who enter the market, the better we can satisfy those needs as a community of farmers. The better we can fulfill those needs, the better the market will grow. **The goal of this book is to help you succeed in this endeavor.**

Produce Farming - Heirloom Style

"The discovery of agriculture was the first big step toward a civilized life." *~Arthur Keith*

Why raise heirloom produce?

Some people say heirlooms are better because they are open-pollinated, and you can save your seeds. Some people say heirlooms are better because they are more adaptable to local environments. Some people say heirlooms are better for your health. Some people say heirlooms are better for the environment. Some people say heirlooms are better because they are more delicious.

Raising heirlooms is more fun because what you grow is not available from a grocery store. If you are going to spend time, money, and effort, why duplicate what some other person has done? Be original. Be bold.

Raising heirlooms allows growers to be creative while producing something familiar. People have a relationship with the food they eat. In all relationships, there is a need for familiarity and novelty. Raising heirlooms allows people to enhance their relationship with their food while building relationships with their local farmers.

Whatever your interest is in heirlooms and whatever the reason is for your interest is in raising produce, one thing is for sure: raising produce is a great way to start farming.

Since the founding of the United States of America, farming has always been a great way to live the American Dream. Raising produce makes economic sense whether you are trying to reduce your family's living expenses or creating a sustainable homestead or family farm. **Here are ten reasons you should grow heirloom produce:**

1. Raising heirloom produce can be a part-time or small-scale business that can turn into a full-time business.
2. Raising heirloom produce can generate cash flow in as little as 30 days.
3. Raising heirloom produce can involve the entire family in a meaningful way.
4. Raising commercial produce is work, but growing heirloom produce is fun.
5. Raising heirloom produce can make farm work a mission-driven activity.
6. Raising heirloom produce supports bio-diversity.
7. Raising heirloom produce is a way to push back against industrial agriculture.
8. Raising heirlooms is a great way to save small family farms and homesteads.
9. Raising heirlooms makes your farm more exciting and fun to discuss.
10. Raising heirlooms is profitable.

Making your work your mission

"The master in the art of living makes little distinction between his work and his play, his labor, and his leisure." ~James A Michener

At times, farming is emotionally draining. At times, farming is physically challenging. At times, farming will stretch your resolve. It is in these times farming will grow you. When farming becomes your mission, it will never be a job. It will be your leisure.

By raising heirlooms, produce farming can become a mission. Many heirlooms are on the verge of extinction. By planting heirlooms, you can do something meaningful, something passionate, and something useful. By raising heirlooms, you are saving valuable plants from extinction.

By raising heirlooms, your farm business can gain a competitive advantage through differentiation. Selling produce is a business, and as with any business, it is vital not only to be different but also to be different in a more compelling way.

The information in this book will help your business to become more attractive, compelling, and competitive. This book focuses on 25 popular heirloom vegetables with descriptions of 473 varieties. *They are varieties not carried by most grocery stores or by most farmer markets and varieties that will give you an edge in the market.*

Heirloom produce offers 15 benefits:

1. **Heirloom produce is unique.** People are attracted to novelty. If given a choice between approaching a prosaic display of green peppers or a rainbow mountain of peppers, most people will visit the colorful mountain.

The uniqueness of heirlooms is a great conversation starter. By explaining what makes your purple bell pepper (or other heirlooms) superior to the traditional green bell pepper (or conventional produce), you are crafting a compelling story. This compelling story *will sell more produce, making you more money.*

2. **Heirloom produce is delicious.** In the pursuit of creating vegetables that look good, transport well, and are shelf-stable, many modern vegetables lack the full deep flavor of heirlooms. According to George DeVault of Seed Savers Exchange, "*Many breeding programs for modern hybrids have sacrificed taste and nutrition.*" Anyone who has eaten a store-bought tomato, blackberry, or peach knows this.

   Our ancestors passed down heirloom seeds for two reasons: productivity and taste. There was no need to worry about storing or transporting during early human history. Our ancestors were more concerned with productivity and flavor.

   As a produce farmer, you are going to compete with the local supermarket and big box stores. The fact is a small farmer cannot produce enough traditional or standard variety produce to compete on price and/or appearance. *Small farmers need something unique, and that something is heirloom produce.*

3. **Heirloom produce is part of human history**. People buy stories. *When vegetables tell a story, customers develop an emotional bond with your farm.* As a business, you are creating a brand. A brand is an emotional connection with a product or service. By retelling an heirloom's history, you build a storyline that the customer can join in with and appreciate.

   Human history is a narrative. This narrative describes how people evolved from hunting and gathering food to raising food and to building civilizations. Heirloom vegetables provided a valuable resource to allow humans to prosper.

4. **Heirloom produce is nutritious.** WWII marks a shift in gardening practices. Before it, gardeners saved seeds because of taste and nutritional value. As people moved to the suburbs and started buying their food from supermarkets, the need for picture-perfect produce arose -- along with the importance of shelf life and transportation ease.

   Hybrids solved these problems, but at the expense of taste. It is because hybrids required fewer taste-enhancing nutrients and inputs, saving production costs. However, fewer nutrients in mean there are fewer nutrients out.

   Since heirloom vegetables require more nutrients to grow, more nutrients are in the plants' flesh and other edible portions. People and animals then consume the nutrients stored by heirloom plants.

5. **Heirloom produce is safer.** The reason heirlooms are safer is they are non-GMO (genetically modified). Here are some interesting facts from GMOinside.org. Today,

---

*"Let us not forget that the cultivation of the earth is the most important labor of man. When tillage begins, other arts will follow. The farmers, therefore, are the founders of civilization." - **Daniel Webster***

---

genetically engineered seeds account for 94 percent of the soybeans and 72 percent of the corn grown in the US and are "Roundup Ready," or can withstand Monsanto's Roundup herbicide (glyphosate).

If this was not scary enough, a 2008 study in Sweden linked Roundup exposure to non-Hodgkin's lymphoma. A 2007 study in Ecuador found the aerially spraying of glyphosate caused a higher degree of DNA damage in a population, DNA damage that can ultimately lead to cancer and congenital disabilities.

A 2003 study of tadpoles exposed to Roundup in Argentina found a higher incidence of skull, eye, and tail abnormalities. A corresponding study in 2009 study in Paraguay found that women exposed to Roundup during pregnancy were more likely to give birth to babies with skull and brain abnormalities.

No study has connected heirlooms to medical or environmental problems. *They have always been better for people and the environment.*

6. **Heirloom produce is sustainable.** Heirloom seeds are non-terminator seeds. Terminator or suicide seeds are genetically modified plants that produce sterile seeds. The idea that someone would create a plant that will not reproduce is crazy and dangerous!

By raising heirloom vegetables and saving your seeds, you can ensure the future of our food supply. By sharing this information with concerned customers, you are connecting with customers in a way that industrial agriculture or grocery stores are unable to connect.

By raising heirloom vegetables, you can sustain a food supply for future generations. The fact that heirlooms exist speaks to their sustainability.

7. **Heirloom produce is vital for maintaining biodiversity.** In the last 50 years, food has become homogenous. Sadly, the days of regional flare and flavor are fading. According to research, diversity enhances the health and function of complex biological systems. Researchers also point out the world of food has become homogeneous.

Some even claim it is approaching the point of a global standard food supply.

In recent years the overall quantity of food has increased. However, there has been a decline in the total number of plant species upon which humans depend for food. With each farm season passing, more people rely on a shortening list of food crops. Plants such as wheat, corn, and soy are taking the place of tomatoes, peppers, eggplants, and many other beautiful vegetables.

Heirloom farmers can change the path. As a farmer specializing in heirloom produce, you are making the world a better place. From a business standpoint, your products are no longer homogeneous commodities when you specialize in heirlooms.

When you specialize in heirlooms, you are creating a valuable branded product. As a farmer, I am amazed at the number of people who bring the same dull produce that you can buy at the local supermarket to a farmer's market. It is refreshing to see the number of people who get excited when they see something new at my market table.

8. **Heirloom vegetables are vigorous**. The natural genetic variation within heirloom vegetable plants makes them adaptable to various conditions. Therefore, heirloom plants can withstand threats such as climate change, disease, and pests.

Heirloom varieties are open-pollinated; unlike hybrids, you can collect their seeds from year to year to produce plants with the most desirable parent plant characteristics.

9. **Heirloom produce is good for the environment**. Chemical and seed companies like people to believe that heirloom plants are more susceptible to pests and diseases. These people like people to think their scientifically designed plants better resist these threats. When, in fact, the opposite is true. *Heirloom varieties grown in the same location year after year will naturally adapt to regional conditions*, creating a safeguard against pests, diseases, and changing environmental conditions.

10. **Heirloom produce is popular.** Heirloom produce creates a culinary adventure. For customers, it is an encounter with prodigious flavor. It offers a striking array of shapes, sizes, colors, and uses, allowing customers to experiment and try new things while allowing you to create an emotional bond with your customer.

    Heirloom produce elevates typical produce from ordinary food produced and eaten for basic survival to a culinary delight. Heirloom produce is not just for affluent consumers or high-end restaurants, but heirloom produce is for everyone to experience.

11. **Heirloom produce is non-uniform.** Uniform vegetables have many limitations. In 2013, The Washington Post published an article titled, *"Why perfect-looking produce*

can be less than ideal." The basis of this article is that perfect-looking produce is not perfect. Picking produce before it is ripe helps it to look perfect, but it ruins the flavor. Besides, the USDA mandates produce sold in stores to be 90% blemish-free. To meet this goal requires growers, shippers, and sellers to sacrifice taste and nutrition for looks.

Heirloom produce comes in many shapes, sizes, flavors, and it ripens over time. Some people claim that heirloom produce is not as pretty as hybrids. Some people claim that the imperfections of heirlooms make them more attractive. However, everyone agrees that heirlooms taste better than hybrids.

Heirlooms struggle as they grow. This struggle increases sugars, antioxidants, and micronutrients--all the things that enhance flavor and health benefits. That is why heirlooms are imperfectly perfect.

12. **Heirloom produce is adaptable**. Heirlooms are open-pollinated, and as pollinators spread pollen, they are spreading the best traits for the area. *The adaptability comes from growers saving seeds from the best fruits from their best plants.* Farmers have their own farming style and methods of production. The seeds saved by individual farmers will be the best seeds for the farmer's growing style, local conditions, and customer preferences.

13. **Heirloom seeds are more economical.** Buying seeds is an expense, and heirloom seeds are more expensive than hybrid seeds in the beginning. However, in evaluating the price, one must consider not just the seed's cost but the money saved in fertilizer, pest control, and weed control. *Growers can also treat these seeds as a source of revenue.* For Example, Jere Gettle from Baker Creek Heirloom Seeds started his company by selling just a few types of seeds when he was a kid. Each year Jere would sell more varieties to more people, and now he has a seed empire.

14. **Heirloom produce is good for brand building**. Brands define businesses. By definition, a brand is a business's identity, and your brand is your connection with your customer. *A brand is your most important asset.*

    By focusing on heirloom produce, you are better able to stand out in a crowded marketplace. As a small farmer, you compete with large multinational corporations with unlimited budgets with departments whose sole responsibility is brand and marketing management. If you are a new farmer, you are competing with established growers who have established customers. Heirloom produce is a way to stand out in this crowded environment.

15. **Heirloom produce is profitable**. Without profit, you will go bankrupt. People farm for many reasons. Some

people farm because they like old-fashioned hard work. Some people farm because they want to connect with the land. Some people farm because they want to get away from the city. Some people farm because it involves the entire family. Some people farm because they are passionate about their products. One thing all these people have in common is they must make a profit.

The farm-to-table movement has created an opportunity for small farmers to make a good living. Today's farm-to-table customers and connoisseurs are actively searching for heirloom produce. *These people are not price-sensitive,* and on average, they have higher incomes, higher education levels and are willing to spend a little extra for the food they want.

24 Heirloom Produce Marketing Tips

Marketing Tip #1. Build a brand. A brand is much more than a logo, symbol, or some sort of mark. *A brand is an emotional connection with customers*. A brand is all the qualities that make a business stand out. A brand is the sum of any business.

Heirlooms provide a pathway to effective brand building. The uniqueness of these vegetables is a way to create a brand for your farm. **Heirlooms are brand builders for three reasons:**
1. People are attracted to nostalgia.
2. People are attracted to quality.
3. People are attracted to uniqueness.

Branding is the most critical business activity. *It communicates quality products and services, promises customer service, and attracts customers.*

Marketing Tip #2. **Do your homework.** To be successful as an heirloom grower, you need to know your target market's location, who makes up that market, and what they want.

The location of your target market is essential. Are you going to sell from your farm, a roadside stand, farmer's markets, or elsewhere?

Many growers start with farmer's markets. Making plans must include visiting as many farmer's markets as possible. Use the internet to guide this endeavor. Pick locations with the best reviews, the most likes, and the best internet presence. Research in advance! Some markets have waiting lists or mileage requirements for vendors.

Leigh Adcock, executive director of the Women, Food, and Agriculture Networks, says, *"Every market has its own culture and vibe."* **The market culture is critical**. A market's culture will not change just because a new vendor is showing up.

In some markets, vendors are collaborative and support others; vendors are highly competitive in other markets, and some will sabotage new vendors. I have experienced this first hand! I have built friendships at some markets and learned valuable growing advice; at another market, a grower came to me on my first day there and explained, quite rudely, why he did not think I should be there.

Market Tip #3 – Differentiate your business. What are you going to do better than your competition? Think about what is going to give you an edge. Of course, heirlooms are a great way to start with differentiation but think about promotion, package design, and customer service.

A great way to differentiate is to tell your farm story. This story needs to explain your farm's mission, purpose, and history. People buy into stories, and stories allow people to make an emotional connection. Your story makes you unique, and competitors can replicate your products and services; however, copying the stories is difficult.

Market Tip #4. Be operationally efficient and effective. Develop a system for organizing, transporting, and displaying your products. It is especially true if you set up somewhere such as a farmer's market or roadside stand where time is of the essence.

It is an excellent idea to develop and use a setup and teardown checklist. This list needs to include change, canopy weights, bags, containers, banners, marketing materials, etc. The checklist should guide market packing and setup.

Market Tip #5 - Speed transaction time. Serving more customers means bringing home more money. The goal is to speed up transaction time without sacrificing customer service. To speed up transaction time, use a waist apron, cargo pants, and keep pricing simple.

A 3-pocket waist apron can speed up making change by keeping change right in front of you. The main pocket of the apron should be the home of the ones, fives, and tens. In one of the other pockets keep quarters, and store large bills in the remaining pocket.

The cargo pants should be for excess cash, pens, phone, or extra items. When pricing items, keep it simple. Everything should be even dollar amounts and give discounts on multiple products based on fives or tens.

Market Tip #6 – Make Connections. At any farmer's market, some vendors have people who always buy from them. These relationships take time to develop, but these bonds provide a steady supply of loyal customers. People want to know why you started farming, your farm products, and your story.

Connect with other farmers at the market. A good farmer's market will be a community of growers. At some markets, there is a second market at the end of the day where people share and trade leftovers. At the very best markets, there are no leftovers, and vendors swap stories.

Market Tip #7 – Think of the customers' experience. Put yourself in the place of your customer. *Your customer's experience builds the perception of your farm.* The customer experience includes displays, quality products, and human interaction.

Always be asking yourself what you can do to improve the customer experience. Greet people! Stand and be ready to say hello or mention the beautiful heirloom tomatoes you have for sale. Do not sit in a chair and stare at your phone – unless you don't want to make many sales that day.

Market Tip #8 - Sell out of abundance. Displays need to be overflowing and inviting. Keep displays stacked or at an angle to keep produce visually appealing. Use smaller boxes as larger boxes become empty. Mix and match products to keep boxes full. Remember the adage, **"Stack it high and watch it fly."**

Market Tip #9 – Avoid Ambiguities. Always state prices, variety types, and other relevant details on each box or display. Some people use clothespins attached to baskets with prices. Some people use chalkboards. Some people write on the baskets. Customers will move to the next vendor instead of asking about price.

Market Tip #10 – Merchandise Effectively. Your farm's logo needs to be on everything and everywhere! Put it on your canopy, vehicle magnets, and farm swag. When selling, everything should have your farm's name/logo on it.

Market Tip #11 - Focus on Visual Appeal. Color moves products, and colorful displays attract attention. Color communicates freshness, taste, and overall quality. *Heirloom produce is available in a wide range of colors and shapes,* making it more visually appealing than other produce. Keep color in mind when organizing your display.

For example, avoid putting cucumbers and zucchinis together and instead put cucumbers and tomatoes together. The contrasting shapes and colors are less confusing and more inviting. *Never create a situation where customers will confuse different types of produce.*

Market Tip #12 - Learn From Others. Always be on the lookout for great ideas. At any farmer's market, someone will be doing something that you can either copy or improve. Look at other people and analyze what they do well and what they do not do well. Business needs to be continually adjusting and adapting.

Market Tip #13 – Greet, Don't Sell. At every farmers' market, there are hard sellers, and there are chair sitters. Neither extreme is profitable. *The best option is to be an active seller.* Active sellers engage people by acknowledging people and allowing natural conversations to develop.

The best strategy is a simple noncommittal greeting such as *hello, hi, good morning, how's your day, thanks for coming out,* etc. It needs to be warm, natural and inviting. No person wants to be in a position of having to commit to a sale immediately.

Market Tip #15 – DIY Marketing. Your farm is your business, and no one cares more about your business than you do. *Take control of your marketing message.* The job of the farmer's market manager is to promote the farmer's market. The manager, at times, may highlight vendors, but it is not their job to make sure you have adequate customers.

Marketing is as important as growing your product. Keep in mind when marketing, people buy stories, connections, and feelings. *Marketing is about treating people like humans and building bridges with as many people as possible.*

Market tip #16 – Use Social Media. A presence on multiple social media platforms is vital. Some apps will manage numerous platforms allowing you to post to one place, and that posting appears on various sites across the internet.

Social media allows sellers to connect with customers on a more regular basis. Social media is a great tool when creating a community around your farm. It enables you to offer specials, move excess inventory, create events, etc. Social media can be a tool when developing customer profiles as well as creating surveys for market research.

Market Tip #17 – Be Mission Driven. Heirloom growers do this by talking about the importance of biodiversity, commitment to improving food choices, and the role heirlooms have played in developing agriculture.

People like to be part of something bigger than themselves, which is a way to tap into that need. There are also customers that value sustainability, and being mission-driven allows you to connect with this demographic.

Market Tip #18 – Provide Samples. Many people are not familiar with heirloom produce, so providing a sample will familiarize people with the superior taste of heirlooms. Providing freebies also show that you believe in your product, and it helps you build relationships.

When providing samples, think about what people are accustomed to eating. For example, many people are familiar with garlic; however, few people know garlic's fresh taste. Choose sampling options that will put your food in the best possible spotlight.

Market Tip #19 – Provide Recipes. It gives customers a visualization tool for how to use your product. Recipes also arouse interest, increase anticipation, and give customers a reason to buy your produce. These recipes need to include your farm's logo, social media information, website, and contact information.

Market Tip #20. Listen to Your Customers. It is an extension of market research. Many customers will talk their way through their purchases, letting you know what they are purchasing and why. It is your opportunity to think about new products to grow, make recommendations, or give suggestions. Most importantly, *listening to customers communicates to customers that you care.*

Market Tip #21 – Price with Pride. Think about how Starbucks prices its coffee (with a lot of pride!). Price your produce the same way. A general rule of thumb is to visit higher-end grocery stores and price your products according to their higher prices for similar products.

Slightly higher than market prices signal quality. Use price as a signal of product supremacy and deliver on that higher quality. Remember, it is always easier to lower prices than to raise prices. Higher prices also give room for price discounts on bulk purchases.

Market Tip #22 – Have a Website. It is incredible the number of small farms that do not have a website. Social media is essential. However, social media places limits on what you can or cannot do. Your website is your platform, and you can do what you want the way you want.

Today, websites are easy to create. There are templates and website builders online that any novice can use. Also, it is easier to take orders on your website, and most mobile sites are just a simple conversion of traditional websites.

Market Tip #23 Package Products Properly. Packaging helps create brand loyalty, and a well-designed package communicates quality. Proper packaging helps with transaction times. Prepackaged products reduce handling time at the market allowing you to serve more customers.

Packaging is a brand extension. People buy with their eyes. Proper packaging appeals to your customer's eyes and feels good to the touch. We all have purchased a product based on its package, and your customers are no different.

Market Tip #24 Develop a Twitter Response. Explain in just a few sentences why and how you farm. In the farm-to-table world, people are more concerned about why you farm and how you farm than what you farm. There is no need to give a dissertation; offer a summary that takes seconds to explain. It is the modern version of the traditional elevator pitch and should last no longer than a short elevator ride of 20 to 30 seconds.

25 Heirlooms for Fun and Profit

Amaranths

Immortal amaranth, a flower which once In Paradise, fast by the Tree of Life, Began to bloom, but soon for Man's offence, To heav'n remov'd, where first it grew, there grows, And flow'rs aloft shading the fount of life. ~ **John Milton**

In Ancient Greece, Aesop compared amaranth and rose. Aesop claimed a rose represents love because of its intense beauty and short life. Amaranth represents friendship because, while less intense than the rose, amaranth is long-lasting and nurturing.

Synchronously and across the ocean, the Aztecs were worshiping amaranth. The Aztecs used amaranth grain mixed with honey to make edible statues of the god Huitzilopochtli. To the Aztecs, amaranth represented sun and war. The sun provides all things necessary for life. War is strength; for the Aztecs, amaranth represented life and strength.

It is no coincidence that ancient civilizations worlds apart appreciated this plant. Amaranth is a pleasing plant. It produces beautiful flowers on tall stalks that are a beacon of hope, beauty, and nature; it serves as an example to the rest of the garden nature's possibilities.

Amaranths is an annual that is useful as a leaf vegetable but used as a grain. The amaranth plant blooms for six weeks before releasing its grains that resemble colorful poppy seeds.

History

Amaranth originated in both the Americas and Europe. This plant has been in production for over 8,000 years. The first Americans to use amaranth was the Mayan civilization of South and Central America, followed by the Aztecs.

Cortez and the Spanish conquistadors outlawed amaranth. The conquistadors believed that by controlling amaranth, they could control the Aztecs. The Spanish nearly wiped out this plant in the New World. Amaranth survived by growing wild and by a few brave people who secretly raised it.

It was not until the 1970s that amaranth had a comeback in North America. Amaranth has been growing in popularity for the past few decades. Today, amaranth sometimes goes by the name the "new quinoa," and people know it is a superfood.

Europe valued amaranth for its appearance. Its use for food was rare. In Europe, it played an important symbolic role as a literary device representing eternal beauty.

Competitive advantage

Amaranth becomes a weapon that small farmers can use in their fight against big Agriculture. *Amaranth is an ancient grain that foodies and environmentally conscious people can get behind and support.* Unlike commodities, amaranth can become a value-added branded product that does not require heavy capital requirements.

Amaranth is better than traditional grains. Amaranth is non-GMO, it is old, and it comes in multiple colors such as purple, red, orange, or green. Amaranth is genuinely unique. A great product to market toward people who are concerned with biodiversity. Amaranth is evidence that a grower is working actively to save plant life, safeguard food security, and protect the environment.

Marketing and Sales Strategies

Many people are looking for alternatives to many modern grains. Amaranth is a great option to offer these people. The key is to market amaranth as an ancient grain that is superior in taste, nutrition.

Aztec celebrations, festivals, and folklore crafts a captivating marketing story. The packaging could include traditional Aztec artwork and design for labels. Using Greek and European legends mixed with amaranth's English literature role is another exciting option that will help create a compelling story. I would not use both. It will confuse customers. *Always remember* w*hen constructing a market message, consistency and straightforwardness moves products.*

Amaranth is naturally attractive. People are attracted to the color and distinctiveness this plant offers. Selling amaranth as a decoration when it is in bloom is one way to generate revenue with this plant. Promoting amaranth as a grain when it goes to seed is another way to generate income with this plant. Amaranth is one of the few plants with two revenue sources.

Production and growing

- **Soil and pH** - Amaranth grows well in various soil types with moderate moisture, but it does require finely prepared soil. The optimum pH for amaranth is from 6.5 to 7.5.
- **Nutrients** - Amaranth is a moderate feeder and does well with compost. If fertilizing, use a fertilizer with high nitrogen (N) and phosphorus (P) content.
- **Water** - Needs moderate watering. Typically, once or twice a week during dry seasons. Amaranth is drought resistant, but its growth will slow during periods of drought.
- **Spacing** - Amaranth needs to 7 to 12 inches between the plants. The closer the plants, the more feed and water required.
- **Growing Temp** - Amaranth does well between 60 to 90 degrees.
- **Pests** - Two most concerning pests are the tarnished plant bug and the amaranth weevil. The tarnished plant bug sucks the fluid out of the plant and stunts seed growth. The amaranth weevil starts on the roots when it is in the larvae stage and works its way up the plant as it grows.
- **Disease** – Diseases are not a common problem for this plant.
- **Hardiness Zones** - Amaranth does well in zones 7 to 12. It does not do well in the north and does better in the Deep South. It requires 120 days of at least 60-degree temperatures.

- **Tips** – Amaranth seeds are tiny. When sowing, mix coarse-grained sand or something similar. It helps to disperse them evenly. Distribute the seeds sparingly across the surface of a finely tilled planting bed and lightly rake them in.
- **Harvest** – Amaranth will continuously flower until frost. Seeds will begin ripening in three months. To determine whether it ready for harvest, gently and briskly shake or rub the flower heads between your hands and see if the seeds fall it is ready to harvest. Amaranth requires no additional processing before use after harvest.

Companion Planting

Amaranth does great with corn because corn provides shade, which will aid with water retention. Amaranth needs lots of nitrogen, so most nitrogen affixing legumes are great companions as well as clover. Pole beans provide nitrogen for amaranth while using amaranth as a trellis.

Vegetable plants such as eggplants and other nightshade plants have similar soil requirements and usually do well together. It helps by increasing resistance to difficult pests while increasing yields, especially with potatoes. Lastly, amaranth is a soil loosener that benefits root vegetables such as parsnips, beets, carrots, and radishes.

Uses

Amaranth is a complete protein that is high in fiber, iron, and calcium. It is a replacement for cereal grain and cooks like wheat berry, cream of wheat, barley, quinoa, or other grains. It may be popped like popcorn and then used to top soups, salads, or used in the same way as sesame or poppy seeds. Amaranth is a thickening agent that is a replacement for cornstarch.

Amaranth's spinach-like leaves are edible and high in vitamin C, according to WebMD. These leaves can be cooked or used raw. Holistic medical professionals use amaranth to treat ulcers, diarrhea, and swollen mouths and throats. Also, it is useful when treating high cholesterol.

Fun Facts

- Amaranth oil prevents and treats cardiovascular diseases.
- Amaranth is the main ingredient of "dulce de alegria," a sweet puff style candy from Mexico.
- Amaranth was first cultivated by the Aztecs 8,000 years ago and is native to Peru.
- The Catholic Church and Cortez once banned amaranth because of its use in religious rituals by the Aztecs.
- Aztec people would make statues of the warrior god Huitzilopochtli out of honey and amaranth.
- Amaranth goes by the name "Chinese spinach."
- Amaranth is gluten-free.
- Amaranth can grow up to 6 feet tall.

- Amaranth comes in at least 60 different varieties.
- Amaranth still grows in the wild.
- Amaranth produces up to 60,000 seeds from a single plant.
- Amaranth produces a half-ton of grain per acre.
- Amarnath is also known as pigweed.
- According to FSR magazine, Amaranth's use in high-end restaurants increased by 19.4% between 2016 – 2017.

Selected Varieties

Aurelia's Verde Amaranth is a native of Guatemala. This variety has light green flowers. It is rich in vitamin B, vitamin A, vitamin E, and iron. Once thought extinct, the Aurelia family saved these seeds. It is returning to its Mayan roots in Guatemala.

Aurora Amaranth is a tricolor variety with creamy yellow upper leaves and bright green lower leaves. It is a smaller variety growing only 2 feet tall and thriving in hot weather. This variety is popular in flowerbeds, containers, or as a garden border. It is edible, but it is not as productive as other varieties. For marketing, this variety is good to sell as a potted plant or seedling.

Autumn Pallete Amaranth is a multicolor plant that inspired Greek legends and early European stories. It is a perfect mix of red, yellow, cream, and green colors with broad spiked blooms. This plant grows up to 4 feet tall with beautiful tassels. The best use of this plant is as a backdrop for flowerbeds and privacy fences.

Bigelow's Amaranth is a New Mexico, Texas, and Louisiana native. Botanical Gazette first documented this variety in 1894. These seeds are hard to find, and some growers try to collect wild seeds. It is a productive variety that is easy to grow.

Burgundy Amaranth is ornamental and productive. It is one of the best eating amaranths. It has a nutty taste that brings salads to life, and the deep red/purple colors are a great contrast to salad greens. This plant grows up to 6 feet tall, providing lots of leaves and seeds for eating.

Dreadlocks Amaranth is a small ornamental variety that produces a mountain of magenta/burgundy blooms that look like a weeping plant with tassels. This plant grows to about 3 feet tall. The leaves and seeds are edible and delicious.

Giant Orange Amaranth is an ornamental plant that grows up to 8 feet tall. This plant produces enormous orange heads. This plant can produce up to one pound of seeds, and the golden stems are edible. A great variety that is tasty, productive, and beautiful to display.

Green-stripe Amaranth is a southwestern and northern Mexico native. This high-altitude plant grows best at elevations between 3,200 – 5,000 feet — a rare plant needing saving.

Green tails Amaranth is a striking plant that grows to 5 feet tall. Since it looks good fresh or dried, florists use this to create vivid displays. The grains are a good substitute for poppies or sesame seeds. It is an easy-to-grow dual-purpose variety.

Hopi Red Dye Amaranth is a dual-purpose variety that grows 7 feet tall. The flowers/heads of this plant look like rope tassels and are perfect for cutting and displaying. The high protein red seeds of this variety make great gluten-free flour, and the colorful leaves work great as greens.

Illumination Stunning Amaranth is a crimson and golden orange variety with sturdy columns of bright green leaves. This plant grows up to 4 feet tall with edible leaves. This ornamental variety is also known as "summer poinsettia."

Love Lies Bleeding Amaranth is a stunning accent plant popular for beds, borders, or containers and is one of the more popular varieties available. This variety grows 3 to 5 feet tall and produces a rope-like tassel of bright red blooms. The flowers are excellent for cutting or drying, and the foliage is edible and highly nutritious.

Marvel Bronze Amaranth is a deep burgundy variety that grows up to 5 feet tall. This flower is long-lasting but will eventually produce a great-tasting seed. The foliage is delicious and nutritious. Marvel Bronze is a great item to combine with white and other light color flowers. An excellent producer.

Molten Fire Glowing Amaranth is a crimson-maroon-colored plant that grows 4 feet tall. The bright red leafy parts of this plant are used as greens and make salads more attractive. This plant defies heat and humidity by producing flowers and foliage until the frost.

Perfecta Amaranth is a medium-sized plant that grows up to 5 feet tall. This plant has scarlet and yellow leaves. As the name implies, this is a perfect variety. It is beautiful and makes a great garden plant, cut flower, or grain.

Southern Amaranth is an annual native to many southern states of the United States. This plant ranges in height from 3 to 10 feet.

Purple Amaranth is an annual Mediterranean native that has spread worldwide, including eastern North America. The seeds are used as grains, and the leaves and shoots are steamed or boiled and then served with olive oil, lemon, and salt.

Artichoke

"At least you'll never be a vegetable - even artichokes have hearts."
~ **Amélie Poulain**

Artichokes have heart and represent hope, strength, and peace -- the three things that move civilization forward. Hope is why we plant gardens, trees and have children. Strength provides resolve and determination to make it through the hard times. Peace allows humans to work cooperatively with each other and nature.

The artichoke is a perennial from the thistle family. It is native to the Mediterranean and the Canary Islands. Artichokes have deep roots that extend four feet or more into the soil, helping prevent soil erosion. Artichokes are suitable for your soil, the environment, and the marketplace.

History

Many scientists believe artichokes descended from the wild cardoon that is a native of North Africa. This wild plant is sturdy, thistly, and hardy. Gaius Plinius Secundus, a Roman naturalist, called it an exciting thistle with a single stem, purple flowers, and delicious fruit.

Romans believed this single stem plant offered many beneficial medicinal effects, including curing baldness, strengthening the stomach, freshening the breath, and promoting boys' conception. Also, the Romans believed the artichoke to be an aphrodisiac. Romans would pickle artichokes or cook them with honey.

As the Roman Empire spread, so did the artichoke. From Europe, the Artichoke made its way to Central and North America. It wasn't until the mid-1900s that the artichoke became popular in North America. Today, artichoke is common nationwide, with 90% of all artichokes grown in California.

Competitive Advantage

California grows nearly all the artichokes in the United States, and you can be sure that not many local producers produce this product (unless you are in California). Many people do not grow artichokes because it takes five years to fully mature and reach optimal production.

Many people look at the time it takes to establish artichokes as a reason not to grow it. For long-term thinkers, however, this is an opportunity. Given the different types of artichokes and most growers raise the same variety, any variation distinguishes your product. Lastly, it is almost certain you will be the only producer in your market selling these expensive products in large quantities.

Artichoke sales have been on the rise, and in 2016, according to grocery store reports, artichoke sales increased by 14% representing a 60-million-dollar market.

Marketing and Sales Strategies

It is safe to assume that the average consumer is only familiar with the globe artichoke. To catch the attention of customers, try mixing and displaying purple varieties with green. It will be a great way to start a conversation with customers.

When promoting artichokes, talk about the health benefits as well as the taste. Have color or artistic pictures of dishes that highlight artichokes, possibly bringing samples. As you discuss artichokes, point out how good it looks on any plate and its ability to make any meal more exciting, attractive, and appealing.

Artichokes are a great value-added product. They make a great tasting dip or can be pickled. Dips are popular for entertaining, lunch, or a snack. Pickled artichokes have a long shelf life and reduce any waste from unsold artichokes.

Production and growing

- **Soil and pH** - Artichokes do best in full sun to partial shade. The soil needs to be fertile, well-drained, sandy, or loam style. The ideal soil pH for artichokes is 6.5-.7.0.
- **Nutrients** - Artichokes do well with high-nitrogen fertilizer or plant food. For best results, fertilize every

other week. If growing organically, use compost with grass clippings, blood meal, coffee grounds, or non-animal kitchen scraps.

- **Water** - Artichokes do best if they have 1 - 2 inches of water a week. Rain water supplies nitrogen and is the best option. The second-best option is fish water irrigation.
- **Spacing** - Artichokes do best when spaced five feet apart.
- **Growing Temp** - Artichokes will germinate when temperatures are 65 - 70 degrees; the ideal growing temperature for artichokes is 60 - 80 degrees. They will grow when temperatures are above 80, but progress will slow.
- **Pests** - Artichokes have few insect pests. However, western pocket gophers will devour the roots. Wire baskets or cages around the plant's base prove to be an effective root protecting strategy. Rabbits and squirrels also love artichokes just as they poke through the ground and are only a few inches tall.
- **Disease** - Artichokes suffer from few diseases.
- **Hardiness Zones** - Artichoke plants do well in Hardiness Zones 7 - 11. They do best in coastal areas with mild winters (50 - 60 degrees F.) and cool (70 - 80 degrees F.) moist summers. However, they may grow in cooler zones but choose varieties that produce buds in their first year or trick the plants into thinking they are in their second year by over-wintering.
- **Tips** – Start seed indoors 6 – 8 weeks before the last frost. "Hardening off" is a process that improves yield and

encourages growth. The plants spend time outdoors before being planted, avoiding harsh winds or torrential downpours. The plants will become visibly sturdier and thicker as you do this two weeks before planting.

*   **Harvest** - Artichokes are ready for harvest when they reach apple size. To harvest, cut the stem below the bud.

Companion Planting

The best companions for artichoke plants have similar soil requirements. **Peas are good artichoke plant companions because they exude the nitrogen that artichokes crave.** Other plants friendly towards artichokes are sunflowers, tarragon, and members of the cabbage family.

Most plants will not hurt artichokes; however, **artichokes have an extensive root system**. It makes it difficult for other plants to compete with artichokes.

Uses

Artichokes are a superfood. The phytonutrients in artichokes provide potent antioxidant benefits. According to a 2006 study conducted by the US Department of Agriculture, artichokes provide more antioxidants per serving than dark chocolate, blueberries, and red wine.

Artichokes are rarely a standalone food; they are typically paired with other food or used in soups, dips, or sauces. Artichokes can be a roasted side dish.

Fun Facts

- Artichokes are one of the oldest foods known to man.
- Artichokes are the only edible thistle.
- Artichokes symbolize peace in many countries such as Libya, Egypt, and Somalia.
- Artichoke is the official vegetable of California.
- Artichokes are a significant source of vitamin C, folic acid, and magnesium.
- Artichokes are fat-free.
- Artichokes have 25 calories per medium artichoke.
- There is a yearly artichoke festival in Monterey, California.
- According to the Greek myth, the first artichoke was a beautiful young mortal woman named Cynara who lived on the Aegean island of Zinari. Zeus turned her into an artichoke.
- Caterina Maria Romula di Lorenzo de' Medici introduced the artichoke to France.
- The origin of the word "artichoke" was most likely the Arabic word *al-hursufa*, possibly meaning "stump."
- European royalty believed artichokes were aphrodisiacs.
- In 1948, Castroville's first "Artichoke Queen" was Marilyn Monroe.

Selected Varieties

Baby Anizo is a light red or purple variety. It is one of the smaller artichokes. At maturity, it is only one inch in diameter. Its attractive color and size are a great conversation igniter. As with most "baby" artichokes, it can be cooked and eaten whole as a tasty appetizer.

Classic Green Globe is sometimes called the "globe." It is the traditional artichoke found in most grocery stores. A delicious variety because of its buttery-tasting heart. The large bottom provides an ample amount of meat at the petals' base. This artichoke ranges from three to five inches in diameter. It is an excellent item to grow and displays well with other varieties.

Siena is approximately four inches in diameter. An Italian variety with a tiny red wine choke. It is a slow grower, and this baby artichoke weighs less than a pound and has a tender heart—an excellent selection to market to avid cooks who want a new twist on something familiar.

Purple of Romagna Artichoke is popular among chefs and foodies. The purple color livens up culinary dishes and farm stands. This variety does better in warmer climates, but northern growers can be successful with a hoop house. It is a profitable option for growers that want an exciting and attractive product mix.

Violet de Provence Artichoke is a purple artichoke that is a French heirloom. The flavor is classic French, and the buds are very ornamental. In France, this is a popular item in gardens. It is rare outside of Europe.

Asparagus

*"You needn't tell me that a man who doesn't love oysters and asparagus and good wines has got a soul or a stomach either. He's simply got the instinct for being unhappy." ~ **Saki***

Through the ages, asparagus has represented prosperity, luxury, and abundance. Asparagus takes time, care, diligence, planning, and work to produce. The same qualities it takes to be successful.

Asparagus is famous worldwide. Its perfection takes time (three years to maturity). It is worth the effort. The result is a culinary delight that is bright, clean, and with an earthy undertone.

Asparagus is dioecious, meaning it has male and female reproductive systems on individual plants. Female asparagus forms red berry-like seeds and produces smaller flowers. Male plants have thicker and larger spears than females with larger flowers.

History

Humans have been growing asparagus for at least 4,000 years. The Chinese and Egyptians were the first two civilizations to develop and use asparagus widely. China used it for medicinal reasons, and Egypt used it in religious rituals.

Hippocrates used asparagus to treat diarrhea. The Romans used it for gastronomic issues, and the Romans ate asparagus both as an entrée and as a side dish. The Middle Ages was problematic for asparagus. Many western Europeans considered asparagus vulgar and a vegetable sent by the devil.

During the 16th century, asparagus made a comeback. During this period, asparagus made its way to the dining tables of the royal courts. Louis XIV ordered his gardeners to grow asparagus. During the 18th century, asparagus became mainstream in Europe, and during the 19th century, it finally made its way to the New World.

Competitive Advantage

Raising asparagus, especially heritage varieties, provides a healthy and tasty product for consumers. This vegetable is popular with people who are health conscious as well as food lovers and connoisseurs. *Asparagus comes in green, white, and purple*. Grouping the three colors makes for an attractive display.

It does take a while to get asparagus started and to start producing. Many producers want quick and easy to grow products, and they avoid asparagus. Producers who grow asparagus can take advantage of other growers' reluctance while developing a crop that can produce for up to 25 years.

Asparagus is gaining ground in the produce departments across the country. It is clear evidence that there is a demand for asparagus. More and more consumers pay attention to this healthy item whose higher price point makes it a winner for growers.

Marketing and Sales Strategies

It is safe to assume that the average consumer is familiar with the green variety of asparagus. **To catch the attention of customers, mix and display bunches of purple and white varieties.** When merchandising asparagus, keep it moist but not wet. If it sits in too much water, it will rot.

Display asparagus in bundles or bags. As you set out your display, organize asparagus next to more brightly colored vegetables that pair well with asparagus for a meal. Think about items such as red potatoes, eggplant, onions, peppers, or carrots. Asparagus is great on a grill, and savvy marketers promote it this way. Asparagus season is February to June, with April being its peak.

When promoting asparagus, talk about the health benefits and taste. Try to anticipate the questions your customers will have and bring photographs of dishes that highlight asparagus. If you see asparagus highlighted in a cooking magazine or a local newspaper, save the article in a binder that highlights it and uses lesser-known plants and vegetables.

Production and growing

- **Soil and pH** - Asparagus does best with sandy, well-drained loam with lots of organic matter and compost. The optimal pH for asparagus is 6.5 to 7.0.
- **Nutrients** - Asparagus is a heavy feeder requiring a steady supply of nitrogen (N) and phosphate (P). A 5-10-10 fertilizer works best.
- **Water** - Asparagus needs water, but not standing water. For best results, it requires 2 to 3 inches of water each week.
- **Spacing** - If growing in beds, asparagus should be 12 inches apart. If in rows 15 to 18 inches apart and the rows should be spaced 3 to 4 feet apart.
- **Growing Temp** - Asparagus grows when the soil temperature is 50 degrees or higher. Optimal growth requires temperatures between 75 to 85 degrees during the daytime and 60 to 70 degrees during the evening.
- **Pests** – Two most common pests are the Asparagus beetle and the Spotted Asparagus beetle. Both pests will feed on the spears and may cause browning or scarring. Some asparagus spears will bend over into a "shepherd's crook." Other pests may include the Asparagus Aphid, Japanese beetle, Cutworms, Armyworms, and other common garden pests.
- **Disease** - Three common diseases for asparagus are Crown & Spear Rot, Fusarium Wilt, and Rust.
- **Hardiness Zones** - Asparagus does best in Zones 3 – 8.

- **Tips** - When growing asparagus, eliminate all weeds from the bed by digging it over and working in a 2- to 4-inch layer of compost, manure, or soil mix. Plant crowns 6 – 8 inches deep. Asparagus does best when raised in a bed and staggered 12 inches apart.
- **Harvest** – Asparagus is best when harvested when the stems are 5 to 8 inches long and when spears are 3/8" thick. To harvest, cut the spear 1/2" below the soil surface. Heads should be tight and spears brittle. Stop harvesting when stalks are less than 3/8" thick. The width will vary from male to female plants.

Companion plants

Asparagus gets along well with many plants, but tomatoes are an excellent companion. Tomatoes repel asparagus beetles, and asparagus repels nematodes, giving each plant a mutual benefit. Early crops such as lettuce, greens, beets, and similar items do well as they are not competing for resources.

Asparagus and artichokes need separation. The root system of the artichokes will crowd out asparagus. Asparagus should not be around other perennials because there will be too much competition for nutrients and growing space.

Uses

Asparagus is a versatile food. It can be grilled, roasted, sautéed, used in soups or salads, or eaten raw. Asparagus is the food equivalent of blue jeans. It is comfortable and goes with just about everything.

This superfood is suitable for pregnant women, people worried about heart health or concerned about osteoporosis. Asparagus is an excellent source of fiber, vitamins, and calcium. Asparagus is used for skincare by applying directly to the skin.

Fun Facts

- Asparagus was considered a phallic symbol banned from girls' schools in the 19th century.
- Asparagus is a good source of folate, vitamin K, iron, and fiber.
- Asparagus can help strengthen blood vessels.
- Oceana County, Michigan, is the self-proclaimed asparagus capital of the world.
- China leads the world in asparagus products.
- Sea salt and asparagus is a herbicide.
- Asparagus plants exhibit sexual differentiation.
- The emperor Caesar Augustus would bark "Velocius quam asparagi conquantur!" or "Faster than cooking asparagus," which means, "Get going already!"
- In the Netherlands, asparagus represents luxury, prosperity, and abundance.

- Pharaoh Ikhnaton and his wife Nefertiti declared asparagus the food of the gods.
- White asparagus turns white from lack of photosynthesis. Growing any variety in the dark makes a white version, which is more expensive.

Selected Varieties

Jersey Asparagus – Is from the Garden State. This variety is vigorous and does well in cooler climates. It has above average resistance to common asparagus diseases such as crown rot, rust, and fusarium wilt.

Mary Washington Asparagus is an heirloom that produces long, deep green spears with pale purple tips. This early 1900s variety has been popular for over a century.

Precoce D'Argenteuil' Asparagus is a popular European heirloom. It has sweet stalks with an attractive, rosy pink tip. It is elusive in North America and not seen in stores. It is almost certain that you will be the only person in the market with this variety.

Purple Passion Asparagus – Is one of the most popular purple varieties. It is an attractive and super sweet variety. It is higher in antioxidants than other types. When cooked, the color fades.

Beans

"Beans have a soul." ~ **Pythagoras**

Whether or not Pythagoras was right is up for debate. What is certain is **beans are good for the soul.** They provide a dependable source of comfort and can drive away the cold – or a cold. A pot of beans can comfort a weary soul and make a person complete again.

Heirloom beans are a great source of protein that will elevate a common commodity to a meal centerpiece. Heirloom beans are a natural leader in the farm-to-table food revolution. They are available in many sizes, shapes, and colors that offer new taste sensations and combinations.

Heirloom beans could be their own book. There are traditional "dry" beans such as pinto. There are butter beans such as Lima, and there are string beans. Within each of these classifications are even more classifications. Virtually every culture in the world has some form of beans as a part of its cuisine.

History

People have been eating beans since the hunting and gathering time. Dry beans were valuable because they could be stored over the winter months or during times of famine. Dry beans were easy to carry. It allowed people to migrate out of Africa and populate the entire world.

The versatility of beans is why it one of the earliest cultivated crops. Beans represented the Egyptian God Ka (or life force), and ancient people carried them on their afterlife journey.

As humans traveled and moved out of Africa and spread to the rest of the world, they carried beans. These beans provided food for the journey and seeds for agriculture.

Competitive Advantage

Beans are productive and easy to grow. Saving seeds from heirloom varieties reduces future seed costs. Not only do heirlooms taste better, but also they come in a variety of colors, including yellow, purple, red, and multicolor.

Beans are critical to France's famous "cassoulet" dish. Cassoulet is a slow-cooked casserole that contains meat, pork skin, and beans. As a farmer, you could find a bean such as the Tarbais or other French variety and package them as a "heritage cassoulet" kit for your customers.

For effective marketing, combine attractive packaging with a great recipe. When your customer makes this dish and shares it with their friends, you emotionally connect with your customer. By selling this product this way, you are not just selling a meal – **you are selling an experience.**

Only a few commercial growers specialize in heritage beans, and those that do tend to focus on one or two varieties at most. **Their reluctance is your opportunity**; by growing something different, you can give people a reason to visit your farm stand, market booth, or roadside tent.

Marketing and Sales Strategies

Beans are popular with a substantial portion of the population. Many people turn to farm-raised vegetables like beans because they are a great protein source at a reasonable price. People with vegan and vegetarian diets use beans as a meat substitute and should be the first people considered when marketing beans.

Chefs who specialize in ethnic, farm-to-table or other trendy foods make a great target market. When talking with these people, discuss unique varieties that could be a meal or novel side dish. The key with this crowd is to offer something tasty, colorful, and profitable.

Dry bean soup kits are a great value-added product. When packaging as a soup, the packaging is more than storing product. **Packaging is an extension of your branding efforts**; it expresses your farm's values, mission, and purpose, and it is a critical part of your marketing efforts. As a customer examines your packaging, it should be clear what the product is, how it is useful, and what needs it will fulfill.

Bean flour is another unique value-added product. Milling bean flour creates a brandable farm product. When selling bean flour, the packaging is critical. People will buy bean flour just because it is different.

Production and growing

- **Soil and pH** – Beans can grow in most soils but do better with loam soil with little fertilizer. The optimal pH is 6.2 to 7.5.
- **Nutrients** - Beans are light feeders and require little food. If beans are over-fertilized, the yields will decrease. Lima beans and pole beans tend to be heavier feeders than other beans.
- **Water** - Beans require little water before flowering, and after flowering, they need 1 inch per week.
- **Spacing** - If growing beans in a bed, pole beans should be spaced 6 inches apart on a 6-foot trellis. Bush beans should be two to four inches apart. If growing beans in rows, pole beans should be spaced out about 12 inches apart, and bush beans should be four to six inches apart. The rows should be a minimum of 18 inches apart.
- **Growing Temp** - Beans will germinate when the soil temperature ranges from 60 - 85 degrees. Optimal growth requires temperatures between 60 - 70 degrees; as the temperature increases, the bean's growth rate decreases. Beans do most of growing during cool nights.
- **Pests** - The two biggest concerns are the Mexican bean beetle and aphids. The Mexican bean beetle is a copper

brown beetle with black spots. Aphids are soft-bodied insects that use their piercing-sucking mouthparts to feed on plant sap. Other pests include the Japanese beetle, Cutworms, Armyworms, among other garden pests.

- **Disease** - Three common diseases for beans are White mold, Bean Rust, and bacterial blight. White mold develops as a white cottony growth on the stem. Bean rust appears as small pale spots (lesions). Bacterial blight appears as small translucent water-soaked spots on the leaf.
- **Hardiness Zones** - Beans can be grown just about anywhere and do best in Zones 3 - 10.
- **Tips** - When growing beans, eliminate all weeds from the bed by digging it over and working in a 2- to 4-inch layer of compost, manure, or soil mix. Do not start beans indoors as they typically do not survive transplanting. Cattle panels make great bean trellises. For a continuous harvest, plant every two weeks and rotate crops annually.
- **Harvest** - Bean harvesting depends on the purpose. Green beans need picking while they are young and tender. Harvesting beans before they mature will extend the growing season; harvest drying beans when the pods turn brown.

Companion plants

Corn and pole beans always go together. Larger sunflowers go well with pole beans. Beans and strawberries do well because the strawberry season ends when bean season begins. Beans also do well with eggplants, cucumbers, peas, and radish.

Do not plant with basil, garlic, or onions. Garlic and onions take a long time to grow, and it is not possible to harvest beans without causing damage to these plants. Also, garlic adds sulfur to soil, changing the soil's pH. Basil and beans attract the same pests and are substile to the same diseases.

Uses

Beans are handy. Their utility ranges from cooking to crafting. Cooking with dried beans has been popular for thousands of years. Most people soak and cook dry beans, but a new trend is bean flour, which the byproduct of ground beans. Bean flour is a thickening agent and gluten-free flour. A benefit of using bean flour is it can transform an incomplete protein (grain flour) into a complete protein.

Beans are in many products such as beanbags, doorstops, draft stoppers, and ergonomic wrist props for typing. Other ideas include counters, tallies, and game indicators ranging from poker to improvised checkers. Lastly, you can make simple percussion instruments and noisemakers from dried beans.

Beans contain a wide range of cancer-fighting isoflavones and phytosterols (cancer-reducing flavonoids). Also, they are high in fiber, which helps fight bad cholesterol. Beans help with weight management because the fiber in beans causes you to feel full more quickly. Proving the adage, "beans, beans - good for your heart…"

Fun Facts

- The Greeks and Romans used the broad bean for balloting—black seeds to signify opposition and white seeds for agreement.
- January 6th is National Bean Day.
- In Nicaragua, newlyweds receive a bowl of beans for good luck.
- Anasazi beans or New Mexico Cave Bean returned to production after sitting idle for 1,500 years in a sealed jar.
- A 1907 Minnesota resolution requires bean soup as a menu option when the Senate is in session.
- The Zolino bean from Tuscany sells for $20.00 a pound.
- The record for the most baked beans eaten with a cocktail stick goes to David Houchin of the UK, who ate 166 beans in 3 minutes.

Selected Varieties

Amish Nuttle Bean – Is a pole bean brought to America by the Pilgrims in 1620. It also goes by the name Mayflower bean. It is a flavorful green bean famous in the Carolinas—a great bean with a great story that will be good for any market.

Anellino Yellow Bean – Is an Italian pole bean that Green Anellino and Shrimp Ring Bean. It is a crescent-shaped yellow bean with delicious flavor and excellent texture. Anellino beans are in high demand by gourmet chefs and are quite rare in North America. A fast-growing bean with only 75 days to maturity.

Arikara Yellow - Is a bush bean with a very patriotic past. This bean traveled with the Lewis & Clark expedition through the winter of 1805 at Fort Mandan. Lewis obtained seeds from the Arikara Indians, and later, he brought seeds to Thomas Jefferson, who added them to his Monticello garden.

Bernard McMahon popularized this bean when he offered it in his 1815 catalog. This dual-purpose bean can be used green or dried for soups, stews, or baking.

Aztec Cave Bean – A recent botanical found during the 1980s. It spent 1,500 years hiding in a cave. Scientists planted them, and miraculously a few grew! It brought life back to an ancient bean, a true comeback story. It is still rare but growing in popularity. The backstory for this bean provides a great selling point for people interested in biodiversity or sustainability. It also goes by the name New Mexico Cave bean, Anasazi, or the 1,500-year-old bean.

Blue Coco – Is a French pole bean that goes by the names Purple Pod or Blue Podded Pole. The Blue Coco is one of the oldest purple-podded pole bean varieties continuously cultivated. This bean dates to the 1700s. It is a fleshy, slightly curved bean with flattened pods range from 6 to 7½ inches long. It is a good source of protein, giving it a pleasant meat flavor. This bean matures in only 60 days and thrives in hot and dry conditions.

Cherokee Trail Tears Bean - Also known as Cherokee Black, is a bean carried by the Cherokee Indians from Georgia to Oklahoma. It is a friendly black pole bean that makes a good snap bean. This bean almost went extinct, but Dr. John Wyche (1911-1985) saved it from extinction.

Corn Hill Bean - Is an Amish bean. The Amish interplant this with corn or sunflowers. A good choice for urban farmers that require compact growing. The beige bean is small and semi-square with rose splashes or speckles on one end. An excellent baking bean that does well when making stews or soups. It is a slower maturing bean taking 95 days to grow, but it is worth the wait.

Hidatsa Beans – A pole bean from the Hidatsa tribe. This productive bean helped this tribe move from location to location. Usually, it is used as a dry bean and has great storability; this red bean does well in dishes such as red beans and rice. Native American dishes are becoming popular, and this Native American bean fits that niche nicely.

Scarlet Runner Beans- A pole bean from Central America, it also goes by the names Oregon lima bean, aycoctl, or ayocote. Many people grow this attractive bean for decoration. It is a versatile and delicious bean that is excellent for salads but takes on a creamy texture when in stews and soups.

Beets

"I'm a beet freak. I put them in the pressure cooker."
~ *Julia Child*

Beets are underappreciated, underutilized, and undervalued. When instead, their uniqueness, utility, and usefulness should be their defining features. They are genuinely magnificent plants. They are unique, offer utility and usefulness. Beets are more than some root eaten on rare occasions; *beets are a celebration of love, passion, and beauty.*

The Romans valued beets. According to historical records, the ancient Romans, beets were worth their weight in silver. Apollo and goddess Aphrodite received beet sacrifices in hopes that their followers would find love.

Beets are biennial plants that are usually grown annually. The beet is similar to turnips or mustard greens but superior in taste and nutrition. Technically, the beet is the green portion of the plant, and the root is the beetroot. When most people say beet, they mean beetroot.

There are four main beet groups: the garden beet with eatable leaves and roots; the sugar-producing sugar beet; the mangel-wurzel, which is easily stored and used as livestock feed; the Swiss chard with its edible leaves and small roots.

History

Beets have been part of the human diet since before recorded history. Beets originated in Mesopotamia and followed human migration to Europe and Asia. Egyptian pyramids and the Hanging Gardens of Babylon both had beets. The ancient Greeks and Romans used beet leaves for wound dressing.

The ancient beetroot was long and thin like a carrot. The modern beetroot began its development in the 16th century. The Scientific Revolution of the 17th century created a pathway for the modern beet and the four current strands.

During Victorian times beetroot became a popular food item to bring color into an otherwise colorless diet. Sugar beets became a standard dessert ingredient. The Victorian era's emerging industrialization made production and distribution more manageable, making beetroots available to more people.

During World War II, beet pickling became widespread, and fresh use declined. As people moved from rural to urban areas, beet popularity decreased. That trend has been changing in recent years as people rediscover the taste and health benefits of beets.

Competitive Advantage

Growing beets gives you two products for the price of one. Growers can sell the greens, roots, or both. Beets are a cool-weather product allowing for an extended growing period and providing an early or late product.

Beets are not a huge seller. However, beets are growing in popularity because of the paleo and primal diet trends. Beets are popular with health-conscious and budget-conscious consumers.

Marketing and Sales Strategies

Beets make a colorful addition to springtime meals. An effective strategy is to promote them with other springtime items such as lettuce.

Beets are a popular juicing item. Their juice offers up the same health benefits as the whole vegetable. Actively promoting beets as a juicing item helps move them. For a value-added item, consider building a new brand of beet juice.

Beets are great for soups. During the fall, market beets with other soup items. Prepare recipes that train customers to think of cooked beets as a hearty side dish as the weather gets cooler.

Production

- **Soil and pH** - Beets do best with sandy loam soil combined with a well-rotted manure and compost mixture to a depth of 8 inches. The optimal pH for beets 6.0 – 7.0
- **Nutrients** - Beets are heavy feeders requiring high potassium (P) but little nitrogen (N).
- **Water** – Beets need damp but not wet soil. Beets have shallow roots and should be water every 2 – 3 days depending on conditions.
- **Spacing** - Thinning will be required. Beets will often produce multiple seedlings when the plant is about 2 inches high, "pinch" the plant to ensure that only one plant/root is growing.
- **Growing Temp** - Beets germinate when the temperature is between 50 - 80 degrees. When the weather is above 80 degrees, beets will bolt.
- **Pests** - Four common pests for beets are the wireworm, root maggots, sugar beet nematode, and cutworms. Affected beets have yellowed, weak foliage and tiny storage roots.
- **Disease** - Since beet is primarily a root, it is vital to watch for common root disease.
- **Hardiness Zones** - Beets do well in zones 3 – 9.
- **Tips** - When thinning beets, do not pull the beets but cut the beets. Pulling beets at this time will disturb nearby beets. Avoid rotating beets where chard and spinach

were grown as these plants are closely related. Beets require full sun.

- **Harvest** - Beets are useable at any stage. Typically, beets are anywhere from 1 1/2 to 3 inches in diameter. Beets whose diameter is greater than 3 inches tend to be woody.

Companion Planting

Beets typically do exceptionally well with bush beans because bush beans will follow the beet harvest. In addition to bush beans, beets do well with cabbage as the beets add minerals to the cabbage's soil. Raising beets mixed with garlic helps the beet's flavor. Beets also do well with head lettuce, onions, and mint.

Beets typically do not well with pole beans, and when planted too closely, they stunt each other's growth. Beets and cowpeas both attract the beet weevil, and for this reason, their togetherness is a bad idea.

Uses

Beets make great soups, stews, or salads. As a side dish or appetizer, beets can be roasted, baked, or grilled. Beets add a sweet flavor to meals. When used as a savory application, cook with crushed or coarse salt. Beets come in a variety of colors that not only add flavor but can add vibrancy to any dish.

Beets are in used sugar production. Making beet sugar or teaching people how to make homemade beet sugar is a great way to attract attention and to sell more beets.

Beets have several health benefits. They can treat liver diseases, lower levels of triglycerides in the blood, and lower blood pressure.

Fun Facts

- Dwight Schrute, from the hit TV show The Office, was a beet farmer.
- Beets contain cancer-fighting antioxidants.
- Beets offer some protection against heart disease.
- Beets are high in folate, which can help prevent congenital disabilities.
- Beets used by the ancient Greeks and Romans were not red but either black or white.
- In 1975, during the Apollo-Soyuz Test Project, American astronauts from Apollo 18 shared beetroot soup with Russian cosmonauts.
- According to folklore, sharing beetroots makes people fall in love.
- Beet juice is good for eliminating bad breath.
- Beet juice is good for eliminating hangovers.
- Beet juice is a natural red dye, including hair dye.
- The red beet is high in natural sugar with a sweet earthy flavor, creating a deliciously sweet dessert wine.
- The largest beet ever grown weighed 156 pounds.

Selected Varieties

Albino Beet – This is a gourmet white variety from Holland. It is a sweet-tasting beet without the staining property of its red cousin. It is a high-yielding beet that matures in 50 days. This variety is excellent for boiling, pickling, baking, freezing, and sugar making.

Albina Vereduna Beet – This white-colored heirloom variety originates from the Netherlands and is perfect for soups or baking. This beetroot is tender, and the leaves perform well when treated like spinach.

Chioggia, Candy Cane, or Bassano Beet – This beetroot is red with white stripes similar to a candy-cane. This Italian heirloom variety immigrated to America during the 1840s. Chioggia, Italy, a seaside town south of Venice, is the birthplace and namesake of this beet. I like this beet because of how well it displays at the market.

Crosby Egyptian Beet – This mesmerizing variety is more flat than round. The root is versatile and can be cooked or sliced for salads. The greens are tasty and can replace spinach. A German variety but given an Egyptian name for marketing purposes. It came to the States in the late 1800s with much fanfare.

Crapaudine Beet – Is one of the oldest heirloom varieties available. Many seed catalogs claim this variety has been around for at least 1,000 years; a claim made from an 1885 French book, *The Vegetable Garden*. The name is French for hinge, and this beet looks like a carrot.

This beet is extremely rare, especially in America. Most likely, if you raise this variety, you will be the only person in your market with this carrot-looking beet. In Europe, high-end chefs seek out this beet.

Cylindra Beet – Is a Danish heirloom dating back to the 1800s. It looks like a carrot, and some people use it as one. It is excellent for grilling or roasting because of its size and shape. Seed catalogs also market this beet as Formanova or Butter Slicer. This beet grows up to 6 inches in 60 days!

Yellow Cylindrical - This is a mangel beet variety. Shape wise it is oblong, but not as long as a carrot. It is a yellow to red European heirloom that started as animal feed. Recently, this beet has made its way into culinary circles. It works best for human consumption when harvested young.

Golden Beet – This is a variety from the early 1800s. This beet is a mild-tasting beet with tender greens. This easy-to-grow variety only takes 55 days to harvest.

Vereduna Beet- This is a classic white beet from Holland. In Europe, this beet is grilled or roasted and served as a side dish with seafood or poultry dishes. The leaves are higher than average in vitamins and micronutrients. It is an excellent variety to grow and merchandises well with traditional red beets.

Swiss Chard is a beet that is grown for its leaves. The beetroot tends to be small and not as tasty as other varieties. On the other hand, Swiss chard leaves are some of the most delicious greens. Swiss chard grows in a rainbow of colors, making it extremely popular at farmers markets.

Cabbage

The insufferable arrogance of human beings to think that Nature was made solely for their benefit as if it was conceivable that the sun had been set afire merely to ripen men's apples and head their cabbages. ~ **Cyrano de Bergerac**

Cabbage is a story of survival and perseverance. Cabbage saved millions of Irish from starving to death during the Great Potato Famine. It sustained European peasants during the Middle Ages. It provided the ordinary people with food and nourishment, so they had the strength and hope to dream for a better tomorrow.

When times were hard for civilization, cabbage provided a lifeline. Cabbage needs recognition for its life-saving efforts. Cabbage deserves credit as a versatile food that can accomplish its job whether cooking it or using it raw.

The cabbage family is enormous; it includes red, white, or green varieties. Cabbage is popular with many different cultures especially, Russian, European, and Asian cuisine. Cabbage is a superfood packed full of cancer-fighting vitamins, nutrients, and minerals.

History

Humans have eaten cabbage for thousands of years. However, the Romans get credit for being the first civilization to embrace cabbage and mainstream food.

The Romans used cabbage for many reasons. Most notable was their use of cabbage as a hangover prevention. During the Roman conquest, the Roman Army carried cabbage as they conquered the known world. The Romans used cabbage leaves to bind wounds and as a source of food.

Cabbage stayed in Europe after the Romans left. In Europe, cabbage's popularity increased as it found a home where it was effortlessly grown. In Europe, people ate cabbage in many ways, including raw, cooked, pickled, and fermented. Cabbage was instrumental during the Age of Exploration as pickled cabbage and sauerkraut prevented scurvy, allowing sailors to spend months at sea.

Competitive Advantage

Cabbage is a cold-weather plant. Growing cabbage allows your revenue-generating season to start earlier in the spring and extend further into the fall. According to grocery stores, cabbage sales have been increasing by 3% a year for the past few years, and it will continue to grow as more people discover delicious new recipes for this superfood.

Cabbage comes in many different colors providing an attractive display. For best results, grow different colors for a more lively presentation. Cabbage is a low-carb vegetable for followers of paleo, Atkins, or other low-carb diets. There is always a low-carb diet trending, so there will always be a target market for cabbage.

Marketing and Sales Strategies

Cabbage is a superfood. This fact is a great starting point for your marketing efforts. When marketing cabbage, focus on its proven ability to manage diabetes, its cardiovascular benefits, and its ability to reduce cholesterol.

Cabbage is excellent tasting when prepared correctly. Provide recipes and samples for potential customers. People are nostalgic and traditional fare can tap into this emotion.

Cabbage is an excellent item for cross-merchandising efforts. Things that go great with cabbage are lettuce, salad mixes, onions, carrots, and oriental-style vegetables.

When marketing cabbage during the spring, St. Patrick's Day is a great holiday to remember. Cinco de Mayo is another cabbage selling opportunity as an alternative to lettuce or as a Mexican slaw.

During the summer, cabbage is best promoted as the main ingredient for coleslaw, and be sure to remind customers of this favorite BBQ or picnic option.

During autumn, cabbage is perfect for soups and as slaw for tailgating events. During winter, cabbage is great for spring rolls.

Red cabbage offers a striking contrast to the green variety. Displaying it together with green cabbage creates an attractive display. When displaying cabbage heads, dry and place the heads butt down to create an appealing presentation.

Production

- **Soil and pH** – Cabbage does best with sandy loam soil that drains well. The optimal pH for cabbage is pH of 6.0 - 7.5.
- **Nutrients** - Cabbage grows in organic compost with high nitrogen (N) and potassium (P). The fertilizer needs to be 5-10-5.
- **Water** – Cabbage needs 1 to 1.5 inches of water per week. For tight heads, cabbage needs regular watering.
- **Spacing** - When growing cabbage in raised beds, cabbage should be spaced approximately 15 inches apart. When spacing cabbage in rows, it needs to be 18 inches apart, and each row should be 24 to 30 inches apart.
- **Growing Temp** - Cabbage seeds will germinate when the temperature is between 45 - 95 degrees. The best growing weather is 60 – 70 degrees. Cabbage will bolt when the temperature is above 80 degrees.
- **Pests** – The most damaging cabbage pests are root maggots, cabbage-worms, cutworms, and flea beetles.
- **Disease** – Cabbage is susceptible to various fungus and needs fungicide while growing.

- **Tips** - Use mulch with finely ground leaves or bark to keep the soil moist and cool. Also, keep the ground weed-free. When raising cabbage, rotate it with other non-cole crop plants for two years before returning it to the same spot.
- **Harvest** – Cabbage is edible at any stage, but it is best to wait until the head is firm and let it grow to the desired size.

Uses

Cabbage is a versatile vegetable that performs well when cooked and does equally well when used raw in salads and slaws. Cabbage's versatility appeals to consumers looking for a different texture in their salads and a distinct flavor in their cooked dishes.

Cabbage treats asthma and morning sickness, aids people with osteoporosis, and helps prevent cancer. Holistic practitioners use cabbage leaves with breastfeeding women to relieve breast swelling and pain.

Fun Facts

- The French word "caboche" means "head," and this is where the English name "cabbage" originated.
- Sailors ate pickled cabbage and sauerkraut to prevent scurvy.
- Cabbage is a digestive tract cleanser.

- Cabbage can improve digestion.
- Scott Robb from Palmer, Alaska, grew a 138.25-pound cabbage.
- David Thomas from the UK grew a 51-pound red cabbage.
- Raw cabbage is silicon and sulfur-rich -- two vital minerals that stimulate hair growth and prevent hair loss.
- Cabbage aids in the prevention of macular degeneration of the eyes.
- In Hebrew, the term "Rosh Kruv" (cabbage-head) implies stupidity.

Selected Varieties

Bok Choy – This is a headless variety of Chinese cabbage and is a traditional variety. Bok Choy is a standard item in Chinese cuisine. It is usually cooked with garlic and soy sauce—an excellent choice for any farmer's market.

Brunswick Cabbage is a German drumhead cabbage introduced in the early 1900s. It is an icy hardy variety that is excellent in fall or winter. This cabbage is great for storage— a perfect choice for sauerkraut.

Cour Di Bue Cabbage – This is an Italian ox heart cabbage that produces loose, tender leaves. This cabbage grows to 3 – 4 pounds. It is a good seller in specialty markets. This cabbage was very popular 150 years ago in Europe and can become popular again with a little push.

Cannonball Cabbage – This is a classic-looking green cabbage. This cabbage looks like a mammoth Brussel sprout growing up to 12 inches across. The cannonball produces very tight/firm heads that are great for shredding into slaw or salads. This variety grows up to 30 pounds, and its dense, compact appearance earned it its name.

Early Jersey Wakefield Cabbage – This is a Yorkshire heirloom that made its way to America in the late 1800s. It produces small cone-shaped heads that weigh 3 – 4 pounds. It is terrific for steaming or sautéing.

January King Cabbage – This is a blue-green heirloom cabbage with curly leaves and purple and turquoise tints. This winter cabbage produces a flavorful, crunchy head. The January King weighs 1-pound when fully mature, making it the perfect roasting cabbage.

Koda Cabbage – Is a Polish heirloom that produces firm round heads that are around 3 pounds each. It is popular in Poland as sauerkraut, in soups, or sautéed with sausage. This early variety produces attractive redheads. Koda is excellent shredded in slaws or salads.

Murdoc Cabbage is a northern European variety that goes by the name Weisskraut in Poland. The cone shape of this cabbage makes it great for mechanical processing. This cabbage has thin leaves and is the main ingredient in various regional sauerkrauts.

This cabbage is about 8-inches across at the base. A medium green variety with a cone makes it standout in produce stands and markets. This cabbage grows best in the fall and takes only 80 days to mature.

Napa Cabbage – This is a Chinese heirloom from the Beijing area. It is a cone-shaped variety with thick, crisp leaves decorated with frilly ends. It has a sweet flavor, and its leaves are softer than most other cabbages. In China, it is eaten raw, steamed, or as filling for spring rolls or dumplings.

Nero Di Toscana - Is a loose-leafed Italian heirloom from the early 1800s. This cabbage has deep purple, almost black, leaves that grow up to 24 inches long. This Italian heirloom is popular in Tuscany and central Italy, used in soups and stews. It is one of the most beautiful and flavorful types available.

Portugal Cabbage – This is a popular western European heirloom with a classic green color. This cabbage has a large spread and ribbed leaves. It is a savory style cabbage – a trendy item for Portuguese-style soups.

Red Drumhead Cabbage – This famous heirloom cabbage made its way to the States in the late 1800s. Its red color makes it a terrific and colorful add-in to slaws and salads. This sweeter than average cabbage does great when pickled.

Savoy Cabbage – This is a variety of cabbage with loose, deep green crinkly leaves that turn yellow towards the base. Savoy cabbages have a stout earthy but mild flavor and great texture. The tender leaves make a great salad addition.

Tete Noire Cabbage – This is a traditional French variety that is very rare outside of Europe. It was one of Julia Child's favorite cooking cabbages who liked its deep redheads. It always does well in the fall.

Tropic Giant Cabbage – This is a fresh market heirloom that does well in the south. This cabbage resists cracking, heat, cold, humidity, and head deformation. This variety does well in the spring, early summer, and fall, giving growers plenty of opportunities to highlight an excellent product.

Walking Stick Cabbage – This is a giant cabbage that grows up to 3 feet. When young, its leaves cook well. As it ages, the leaves become bitter and hard. The size of this cabbage is great for garnering attention. It is a good item for growers with roadside stands who have their gardens nearby.

Quintal D'Alsace Cabbage – Is an heirloom from the Northeastern region of France. It has been a fashionable item in French cuisine for over 150 years. The mass of this cabbage has given it the nickname hundredweight. This cabbage is cold hardy, and does well in late fall and early winter.

Carrots

"The day is coming when a single carrot, freshly observed, will set off a revolution." ~ **Paul Cezanne**

Growing carrots teaches many life lessons. For example, carrots teach people the best rewards require digging. They teach people the importance of roots. Carrots teach people that rewards are better motivators than punishments. With their bright colors, they demonstrate the importance of being unique.

People have long thought of carrots as a source of good fortune. For example, people gave carrots to brides for good luck during the Renaissance. Celtics hunters would eat carrots before hunting exhibitions. Sailors would eat carrots before long voyages. Wherever people and carrots coexisted, people believed carrots to be beneficial.

Today, carrots are delicious culinary devices and a superfood. Carrots are a biennial plant, but most people treat them as an annual. Carrots can be ready to market in as little as 90 days. It is a popular food worldwide. Carrots taste great, have health benefits, and are easily stored. Carrots are great raw or cooked.

History

People have eaten carrots all during recorded history. For thousands of years, only white wild carrots existed. The Silk Road carried different varieties of white carrots between the Roman Empire and China.

The intermingling of the different carrot varieties created new varieties. Carrot seeds traveled with traders who exchanged them with people from far away places who grew them in varying conditions. Carrot roots had to work harder in new soils, causing the roots to grow bigger. Some areas were more suited for beta-carotene carrots, which created the delicious orange carrot we all enjoy. Carrots cross-pollinated with related plants, and the result is the kaleidoscope of colors we have today.

For thousands of years, carrots came in black, white, red, and purple. The orange carrot is relatively new and came about as a political statement. The Dutch invented the orange carrot as a tribute to William of Orange, who played a pivotal role in the Dutch Revolution.

Competitive Advantage

Selling red, yellow, white, and red carrots will attract people to your products. *Multicolor displays are always eye-catching* - making your products superior to that of any grocery store.

Currently, carrot sales are increasing by 8% annually. Carrots rank as the fifth-best tasting vegetable according to Ranker Market Research. Carrots are the fourth most purchased vegetable in grocery stores. Baby carrots, which are tiny processed carrots, have been driving carrot growth.

Colorful carrots are a way to compete with baby carrots. They have more vitamins, minerals, and micronutrients; they have a superior taste and a better marketing story. *Colorful carrots are more fun to grow, display, and share with others.*

Marketing and Sales Strategies

Having a rainbow of options allows for great merchandising of carrots. Growing different colors and stacking them high will attract people to your farm stand. There are many value-added products that you create, too. For example, carrot cake, carrot muffins, and with access to a commercial kitchen, you could make premade salads and carrot sticks.

Baby carrots and carrot chips are doing well in the retail marketplace. Both products have gained success by focusing its use as a snack. Interestingly, neither product touts carrots' health benefits but instead focuses on carrots as a dippable snack. Therefore, there is a business case that this is possible on a local level, and there is no reason that a marketing-driven local producer could not develop this niche.

While marketing carrots, think about the juicing options and promote the benefits of carrot juice. Carrots make a great add-on to any lunch box. Do not forget Easter! Carrots and the Easter Bunny should go together like peas and carrots – Easter can provide some various (even cute) marketing opportunities for carrots. *People like products that make life easier, and carrots make an easy snack, side dish, and companion to most meals.*

Production and growing

- **Soil and pH** – Carrots need deep, loose sandy loam-type soil 24 inches deep. The optimal pH for carrots is 6.0 to 6.8.
- **Nutrients** - Carrots do best with composted soil. Carrots need phosphorus (P) for the roots and nitrogen (N) for the tops. Applying phosphorus (P) directly to roots with a drip irrigation system yields the best results.
- **Water** - Carrots require constant damp soil but not wet/muddy soil. Carrots do not tolerate drought conditions and require 1 to 2 inches of water a few times a week during dry periods.
- **Spacing** - Carrots should be spaced at least 1 inch apart in all directions when growing in a bed. The best result is using a grid pattern. When growing in rows, carrots need to at least 1 inch apart in rows wide enough to walk or till through without damaging the carrots as they grow.
- **Growing Temp** - Carrots are cool-season plants that do best between 55 and 75 degrees. Seeds will not germinate above 95 degrees and will bolt.

- **Pests** - The most significant pest would be the root-knot nematodes. Other pests include false wireworms, cutworms, grub worms, and other root-loving insects.
- **Disease** - The most common carrot disease is the Alternaria leaf blight, and it occurs during wet periods in the summer.
- **Hardiness Zones** - Carrots grow best in zones 4 - 10.
- **Tips** - For disease control, practice a three-year rotation with non-susceptible crops. Remove and destroy infected crop residue—plant on ridges to improve drainage and enable the soil surface to dry more rapidly. Carrot soil needs to be free of roots, rocks, and other debris, requiring soil screening. Carrots need planting as soon as the last chance of frost has passed unless growing in a hoop or greenhouse.
- **Harvest -** Being a root, carrots are edible at any time. Picking carrots occurs when carrots are 2 - 3 months old and are about 1/2 inch in diameter. Carrots are ground storable until the first frost.

Companion Plants

Carrots play well with many different plants such as beans, lettuce, onions, peas, rosemary, radishes, and sage. Beans add nitrogen to the soil while the other listed plants break the soil.

Carrots do not play well with dill or parsley because both plants have damaging root excretions. Parsnips and carrots both attract carrot flies and are susceptible to the same soil-borne diseases.

Uses

Carrots have many uses; the most obvious is food. Carrots are a great-tasting superfood with many health benefits. For example, carrots promote eye health, are a great source of antioxidants, protect against cancer, and are good for skin and general healing.

Carrots are great for cooking because they go with any main dish and are a great garnish. Carrots are great for baking items such as carrot cakes and muffins, and they are a perfect juicing vegetable.

Fun Facts

- Orange carrots result from selective breeding during the Dutch revolt to show support for William of Orange.
- Carrots can fight the signs of aging.
- The word carrot comes from Celtic, which means red of color.
- Bugs Bunny's favorite food was a carrot.
- Eating carrots helps remove plaque and aids in the cleaning of teeth.
- Carrots are 88% water and aid in the prevention of dehydration.

- April 4th is International Carrot Day.
- Carrot Sunday is the Sunday before the Feast of St. Michael.
- The Wild Carrot is called Queen Anne's Lace.
- The Celtic's describe the carrot's taste as honey from the ground.
- The botanist, Hieronymus Bock (1498–1554), claimed wild carrots were good for fertility and used his study of wild rabbits to support this claim.
- One medium carrot provides a day's serving of vegetables.

Selected Varieties

Amarillo Carrot is a juicy yellow carrot with a lengthy history. This Spanish variety grows to be 8 inches long. Amarillo carrots contain high carotenoid lutein levels, a pigment like a beta-carotene that transforms into Vitamin A during digestion.

Atomic Red Carrot is a red carrot that gets its color from lycopene, a cancer-preventing antioxidant. This carrot grows exceptionally well in the fall season. It is lovely and matches with yellow or purple carrots. Unlike other vegetables, whose colors fade when cooked, the color of this carrot improves. Slicing this carrot into rings makes an attractive side dish.

Black Nebula Carrot is a purple carrot that takes 75 days to grow. It tastes delicious raw but is often roasted, grilled, steamed, or baked. The stunning color makes meals fun and attractive. This old carrot is an eye-catcher at the market. Some people raise the Black Nebula for its gorgeous flower.

Black Spanish Carrot is purple on the outside and lemon yellow on the inside – making it a striking heirloom. The contrasting color brings excitement to meals or snacks. This carrot came to Spain from the Middle East during the middle ages. It is not as sweet as other carrots and is slightly spicy and earthy tasting. It pairs well with other root vegetables such as potatoes, turnips, parsnips, etc. This carrot is a culinary surprise.

Half Long Carrot is an orange heirloom from the 1870s. It is a highly productive carrot that was the gold standard of carrots for decades because of its flavor. It is a fast-maturing carrot taking only 70 days to grow – an excellent carrot to have in the carrot mix.

Dara Flowering Carrot or sometimes referred to as Queen Anne's lace flower, is often planted as a flower in flowerbeds. The root and flowers of this plant are edible. The flowers are purple, pink, and white. The Dara is a wild carrot that is more ornamental than culinary. The root is small and lacks the flavor of other varieties.

Gniff Carrot is a Switzerland heirloom from the Tessin region. Its purple exterior and white interior create an appealing visual contrast. Europeans pickle this carrot using olive oil, basil, and garlic, which is an excellent idea for a value-added product. It is a very rare carrot with tremendous marketing potential.

Kuttiger Carrot is a 300-year old heirloom from Kuttiger, Switzerland. It is a stocky white carrot that looks like a parsnip. It is a prime choice for market growers because of its storability with ease of transport. This carrot is easy to grow and has a mild and delicate flavor. This carrot has a subtler taste than other varieties.

Koral Carrot has a long history in Europe and is very rare in America. The Koral is a great juicer. It is an outstanding addition to any market grower's product mix. It's an orange carrot that stores well, and it is easy to grow. This carrot is full of carotenoids and sugars, making it both healthy and delightful.

Kyoto Red Carrot is a Japanese heirloom sweet carrot that originates near Kyoto, Japan. A popular carrot for the Japanese New Year. This carrot has a splendid texture and sweet flavor. The bright red color becomes much darker when grown in the winter, a perfect variety for late summer, fall, or winter gardening.

Lobbericher Yellow Carrot is an old European heirloom. Initially, this carrot served as animal fodder. This old-world variety must be harvested young for human consumption, as it turns woody and unpalatable as it matures. This carrot has a mild, sweet flavor.

Lunar White Carrot is a Northern European heirloom from the middle ages. This wild carrot is rare, and the seeds are hard to find. The rarity makes it an attractive item for the product mix. This carrot loses its flavor and becomes woody as it ages. For maximum taste and flavor, harvest while young. The white color makes it a great salad addition.

Muscade Carrot is an orange heirloom from northern Africa. This crisp carrot can grow up to 7 inches long. When mature, it has a woody taste to avoid this harvest it young. This rare carrot is on the verge of extinction and is uniquely good in carrot cake, a profitable cottage good.

Oxheart Carrot is a squatty orange heirloom from France that looks like an orange turnip. It is a good choice for shallow soils. It is slow to bolt carrot that does better in the heat than most other carrots. It's a perfect raw snack because its taste is crisp and sweet. This carrot can be quite substantial - weighing up to a pound!

Pusa Black Carrot is an heirloom from India. This carrot's color is from its extremely high content of anthocyanins. It is a very healthy and great-tasting carrot that does excellent in the south during warm weather. This carrot is a great juicer or slicer.

Pusa Rudhira Red Carrot is an heirloom from India. It is above average healthy carrot because it is high in beta-carotene and lycopene. It is red on the outside and orange/red on the inside. It is easy to grow, store, and tastes better than it looks.

Purple Dragon Carrot is an American heirloom from the 1880s. Many seed companies market using its nickname, the "Red Dragon." This carrot is a purple carrot on the outside and with a yellow inside. This carrot is very hardy and does well in northern climates. This carrot's contrasting colors make it exceptionally attractive when sliced, used in relish, or as a garnish. This carrot has the nutritional value of a tomato — a perfect marketing carrot.

Corn

"Then plough deep while sluggards sleep, and you shall have corn to sell and to keep" ~ **Benjamin Franklin**

Corn provided early Mesoamericans the opportunity to be significant. For these people, corn represented the cycle of rebirth. Each year it allowed people to improve, learn, and grow in each growing year Mesoamericans built upon the previous year's accomplishments. The same thing we should all be doing.

As corn traveled to Europe, it quickly became a universal symbol for abundance, diligence, and rebirth. Corn replaced grain as the metaphor of choice when describing productive endeavors.

Corn is an annual plant ready for harvest in as little as 60 days. Corn is ready for harvest when the ears turn dark green, silks turn brown, and kernels are soft and plump. It is a popular food the world over. It tastes great, is healthy, stores well, and transports easily. There are six basic types of corn.

- **Dent corn**, which is the most widely grown corn. This corn is best for animal feed and industrial applications. Also known as field corn - it contains a mix of hard and soft starches that indent when dried.
- **Flint corn**, commonly referred to as Indian corn or pod corn, is like dent corn. It has a hard shell and grows in a multitude of colors. This corn is decorative.

- **Popcorn** is a type of flint corn but has a specific size, shape, starch level, and moisture content, making popping possible. Popcorn has a hard shell and a soft starchy center. When heated, the natural moisture inside the kernel turns to steam and builds up enough pressure to eventually explode.
- **Sweet corn**, commonly known as "corn on the cob," is a "soft starch" corn with corn's highest sugar content. This corn is edible when kernels are in the milk stage.
- **Waxy corn** was developed in China in 1906. This corn is like dent corn in appearance; however, the starch makeup is different. Standard corn kernels consist of 75% amylopectin and 25% amylose, while waxy varieties are nearly 100% amylopectin. Waxy corn has human consumption uses as well as industrial uses.
- **Flour corn** has a soft exterior and soft starch, making it easy to grind. This old type of corn was a staple food of Middle Americans around 1,200 AD. Ground corn is easy to transport and cook. This feature created many current culinary treasures such as cornbread, corn tortillas, and corn taco shells.

History

Corn is the first human-engineered vegetable. The history of corn started over 7,000 years ago by peoples living in Central Mexico. Corn is unique; there is not a wild version of corn growing anywhere. The closest relative is Teosinte, but this looks more like a traditional grain than corn.

Corn spread from central Mexico to Northern America. Columbus brought corn back to Spain, where it quickly spread through Europe and Africa, and Asia.

Europeans embraced corn. It spread quickly, and you could say it was an overnight sensation. Corn found its way into food as well as into literature. Today, corn is in all regions, making it the most popular food plant to travel out of the new world.

Competitive Advantage

Corn is one of the bestselling items in the produce section of most grocery stores. However, corn production for human consumption is declining as industrial corn producers are growing corn for animal feed or industrial uses instead. This reduction has caused a price increase for sweet corn.

Many people love fresh, sweet corn to the point that they actively search it out. I know that at the farmer's market I attend, sweet corn routinely sells out. *Sweet heirloom corn is an attractive and delicious item to introduce to the marketplace.* Heirlooms provide various colored corns allowing for more creative marking, colorful displays, and captivating narratives.

Corn mazes are a great way to make money with corn. Corn mazes are great as a standalone attraction or in conjunction with a pumpkin patch.

Marketing and Sales Strategies

There are many ways to market corn. Most market growers sell it fresh. Letting corn mature allows it to be a value-added product such as cornmeal or popcorn.

Popcorn is popular, but only a few locally grown producers target the farm-to-table or locally-grown crowd. There is no reason why a small farmer could not create a brand of pop or kettle corn with their farm logo, brand, or image.

When marketing corn, focus on the locally grown aspect. Many consumer concerns are with the industrial production of this commodity. Explain to customers how locally-sourced corn is safer, using fewer chemicals, and is better for them and the environment. Lastly, let consumers taste it. Locally grown, fresh corn will always taste better than store-bought corn – honestly, there is no competition in taste!

Production and growing

- **Soil and pH** - Corn may be grown in average garden soil. The soil needs to have good drainage. The optimal pH for corn is between 5.5 and 7.
- **Nutrients** - Corn is a heavy feeder and needs generous quantities of nutrients, especially phosphorus (P) and potash.
- **Water** - For proper kernel development, corn requires a steady supply of water. The soil should be moist but not wet. Water is most critical during germination, tassel, and silk formation. Corn needs 1 to 2 inches of water a week.
- **Spacing** - Corn needs to be in multiple rows a minimum of 12 inches apart.
- **Growing Temp** - Corn needs three months of warm weather where the temperatures are between 60 – 90 degrees.
- **Pests** – Common corn pests are corn earworm, European corn borer, and Japanese beetle. The corn earworm eats its way into the kernel—the European corn borer tunnels into the stalk. The Japanese beetle gathers on the tip of the ear and feeds on the silks.
- **Disease** - Corn is susceptible to diseases such as corn smut, rust, root rot, stalk rot, and leaf blight. The best prevention is proper crop rotation, seed sanitation, and the appropriate use of pesticides.
- **Hardiness Zones** - Corn does best in zone 4-8.

- **Tips** – Do not transplant corn. Root shock could kill the plant. Where drainage is an issue, plant corn in hills to keep standing water away from the roots, do not plant corn in a single row because it impairs pollination.
- **Harvest** – Pick sweet corn when the tassels turn brown. To get corn off the stalk, use a downward twisting motion; if you are growing corn for value-added dry products, seed, milling, or popping, wait for the husk to brown.

Companion Plants

Corn gets along with many vine-type plants. Corn and beans make a great pairing. For urban gardeners, this is a great space-saving strategy.

Cucumbers pair well with corn. Also, many squash plants do well with corn. Some people will plant corn in between bush-style squash. Corn matures before pumpkins, and growing these items together makes sense.

Tomatoes and corn attract the same pests. Plant these items far apart for their safety.

Uses

Corn is usually a side dish. Options for cooking corn include boiling, roasting, or grilling. When dried, people mill it into cornmeal, cornflakes, or cornstarch.

Industrial uses of corn include corn syrup, oil, and fuel. There are many products made from corn and corn by-products.

Corncob pipes, fertilizer, and animal bedding are made with dried corncobs. Corn stalks are useful as a fed filler, resin, or decorations. Virtually every part of corn has a commercial use or application. Some of the applications may be beyond the technical skills or are not economically viable for a small farmer. Still, other ideas such as handmade corn pipes may provide a unique niche.

Fun Facts

- Corn is a member of the grass family.
- Columbus introduced corn into Europe.
- Corn has 16 rows of kernels.
- Corn has 800 kernels per cob.
- Corn has an even number of rows on each cob.
- Corn grows on every continent in the world except Antarctica.
- Corn is known as maize.
- The Native Americans described corn as the giver of life.
- Choclo is Peruvian corn that has kernels the size of a quarter and is the largest corn breed globally.
- The corn belt includes the following states: Kentucky, Illinois, Nebraska, Ohio, Minnesota, Indiana, Wisconsin, South Dakota, Michigan, Missouri, Kansas, and Iowa.
- There are over 3,000 different uses for corn products.

- A bushel of corn (eight gallons) can sweeten 400 cans of soft drinks.
- Corn is found in many non-food items, including but not limited to paint, shoe polish, ink, cosmetics, plastic, film, rust preventatives, fuel, and as a substitute for other petroleum products as well as many other things.
- Forty percent of America's corn goes to ethanol production.
- Cornstarch forms into plastics, fabrics, adhesives, and other chemical products.
- The first mechanical corn harvester was developed in 1930 by the Gleaner Harvester Combine Corporation.

Selected Varieties

Amish Butter Corn is an heirloom popcorn developed by Pennsylvania Amish in the mid-1880s. This sweet popcorn has a butter flavor and tastes great without salt, butter, or oil.

This corn can be ground and used for masa or flour. This flour is excellent for polenta, tamales, grits, and bread. This superb choice offers many branding opportunities for a small farmer who wants a unique product.

Aztec Black Corn, sometimes called Black Mexican corn, is an heirloom black corn that has been around since the Aztecs. If eating fresh, harvest it when white. If used for flour, it is best to wait until it dries out and turns black. This corn makes for a colorful flour that will make corn-flour products more attractive.

Big Horse Spotted Corn is dark, multicolor heirloom corn from the Osage tribe. The ears of this corn range from 6 - 8 inches long. This dry-use corn is perfect for grinding and milling; it is hard to find but fun to grow.

Bloody Butcher Dent Corn is a Virginian heirloom variety. It is a red-dent corn from the 1840s that grows up to twelve feet tall. The ears grow to be 8 – 12 inches long. This dent variety is sweet, rich, and tastes excellent when ground into flour.

Burro Mountain Popcorn is an heirloom popcorn from central Mexico. The Aztecs used this corn for rain and war ceremonies. This corn is the ancestor to almost all the popcorn grown in the United States; it is scarce and nearly extinct.

Chapalote Corn is a 4,000 year-old heirloom! It is a cross between flint and popcorn whose taste and history connect us to our ancestors. This corn is great for popping or grinding. I have been thinking about growing this corn and making value-added Cahptalote tortillas or Chapalote cornmeal because the name has great marketing appeal.

Cherokee Long Ear Popcorn has a sad history. This corn traveled the Trail of Tears. The Cherokee people's resilience saved this beautiful red, black, white, orange, and yellow corn. Culinary uses of this corn include popping, grilling, baking, or grounding into flour.

Cherokee White Eagle Corn is a very productive and easy to grow Native American heirloom. This decorative corn has white and blue kernels. For eating, it is best to roast when young and to grind as flour when it matures.

Hopi Purple Corn an heirloom from the Hopi nation. This old corn has been in production since 500 BC. It originated in what is now Arizona. This corn performs well in hot and dry conditions. Hopi corn is high protein corn that grows on bushy stalks producing 8-inch ears that people ground into flour.

Indian Berries Popcorn is an ear of squatty multicolor heirloom corn that grows 3 - 5 feet tall. The smaller stalks make great decorative pieces for houses, apartments, or interior decorating. Indian Berries does well when ground into flour. This corn takes 90 days to mature.

Maiz Morado or Kulli Corn is a Peruvian heirloom from the Andes. This corn is dark purple, almost black. The dark color comes from its dense anthocyanins level; it has the highest level of any corn.

This corn is the main ingredient in the Peruvian drink called chicha morada, an integral part of Inca religious ceremonies. Growers could recreate this drink and offer samples as a conversation starter or as an attention-getting strategy. This corn is sweet when it is young and becomes good for grinding as it matures.

Oaxacan Green Corn is a Zapotec heirloom from Mesoamerica; this green corn makes green flour popular for making tamales or cornbread. Grinding this corn into flour and mixing it with red jalapenos and other colorful hot peppers makes cornbread that appeals to the eyes, mouth, and stomach. Try making this cornbread into a value-added product.

Osage Brown Crown is an Ozark heirloom that grows well in Southern Missouri and Northern Arkansas. It is a grinding-corn with dark brown kernels. The stalks are short, growing no more than six feet that only produce 1-2 ears per stalk.

Po'suwaegeh Blue Corn is a Native American heirloom from the Pueblo Pojoaque region of North New Mexico. The Tewa people who grew this corn ground it into a Corn Atole dish, a mush made from ground corn, milk, and water. Corn Atole is an excellent option as a value-added product and is a unique way for customers to sample corn while connecting with the past.

Smoke Signal Indian Popcorn is a multicolor heirloom corn raised by the plain Native Americans. The stalks of this corn were used to build fires to send smoke signals for the fall buffalo harvest. It is productive growing up to 8 feet tall, making it a sturdy trellis for beans or other vine plants.

Stowell's Evergreen Sweet is a New Jersey heirloom. At one point, it was the most expensive corn on the market, with seeds selling for a whopping 25 cents a pint in the late 1800s. This sweet corn stays greener longer in the fields, creating a larger window for harvest. This corn grows 6 to 8 feet tall with 8 to 9-inch ears.

Cowpeas

I'm good in the kitchen; I can cook seafood, collard greens, black-eyed peas. ~ **Monique Coleman**

Cowpeas thrive under adversity. They grow in drought conditions with minimal assistance while producing something tasty and nutritious. There is no wonder that the most famous cowpea, the black-eyed pea, symbolizes good luck during the New Year. The ritual of eating black-eyed peas is a reminder to persevere when things get hard. Hardships are inevitable, but we can be steadfast and grow like the black-eyed pea.

The cowpea takes whatever the environment gives it and does something productive. It doesn't complain and say "if only…" nor does it compare itself to other plants. The cowpea seizes any available opportunity.

Cowpeas are an annual legume that takes up to 140 days to mature. They are hardy and may thrive in poor, dry conditions and growing in soils up to 85% sand. Cowpeas are the most productive when it is warm, and the soil temperature is consistently above 65 degrees.

History

Cowpeas are an old African plant that thrived during the African Humid Period. As the Sahara shifted from grassland to desert, cowpeas adapted to the marginal growing conditions.

As people migrated from Africa, they carried dried cowpeas. This event allowed the cowpea to spread to the Middle East, Asia, and Europe. Cowpeas made it to the Americas during the late 1660s on slave ships.

Slaves grew cowpeas because they were easy to grow. Freed slaves carried cowpeas with them as they re-established their lives. This process earned cowpeas the name *poor man's food*. Fortunately, as poor people prospered, cowpeas did, too. Today, people from all walks of life are searching for the gourmet cowpea – and today's farm-to-fork movement can give them a place to find it.

Competitive Advantage

Cowpeas add diversity to the product mix. Dried cowpeas are a brandable product offering year-round sales potential. Cowpeas pair with many other vegetables such as tomatoes, okra, greens, collards, green beans, and carrots. It allows for many cross-merchandising opportunities.

Soup kits are a great value-added product to use with cowpeas. Soup kits provide something easy for customers to prepare and make great gifts for people; they can allow you to create something with a regional flair. Soup kits are great for marketing giveaways to promote your farm. Most importantly, soup kits will enable you to earn more profits with cowpeas.

Cowpeas offers production advantages. Cowpeas are a tool to create value out of invaluable soil; marginal soil is not a problem for cowpeas, allowing the best space for the more delicate produce.

Marketing and Sales Strategies

Cowpeas offer many marketing opportunities. People like cowpeas fresh, dried, or processed. For fresh cowpeas, offer recipes. For dried cowpeas, offer meal or soup kits, and for processed, offer cowpea soups, canned cowpeas, hummus, or salsa.

Cowpeas are the main ingredient in many southern or soul food dishes. People like events. To sell more cowpeas to more people, consider offering southern or soul food events. Cowpeas are available year-round, making this idea viable. Never underestimate a niche like this; the right product in the right market could increase your farm's viability year-round.

Production and growing

- **Soil and pH** - Cowpeas grow in most garden soils. Cowpeas need a neutral pH or 7.
- **Nutrients** - Cowpea is a nitrogen-fixing crop, so it does not need nitrogen. Cowpeas benefit from potassium (K) and phosphorus (P).
- **Water** - Once established, cowpeas do not need much water. While establishing cowpeas benefit from moist soil with up to 1-inch of water per week.
- **Spacing** – In rows, they need to be 5 inches apart, 18 to 24 inches apart. In beds, cowpeas should be 5 inches apart in all directions.
- **Growing Temp** - Cowpeas do best when the temperatures are above 60 degrees. Cowpeas are frost intolerant, so any frost will kill them. If a light frost doesn't kill, save those seeds because you have something special that needs saving.
- **Pests** - Cowpea curculio, a type of weevil, is a significant problem. Stinkbugs, in general, are damaging to cowpeas, especially young seeds and pods. Other pests include armyworms and beet armyworms.
- **Disease** - Common cowpea diseases include Cercospora leaf spot and choanephora pod rot. Southern blight is a fungus that can cause problems for cowpeas.
- **Hardiness Zones** - Cowpeas do best in southern regions and zones 7 – 10. Cowpeas can grow almost anywhere in North America with 90 days or more of above 60-degree

temperatures. Northern growers need to take care to pick the appropriate variety for their region.

- **Tips** - Cowpeas tend to crowd out weeds and have minor problems. The best advice for cowpeas is to plant them well enough in advance of a frost, so they have time to grow. Planting seeds 1 to 1.5 inches deep yields the best results.
- **Harvest** - Cowpeas are harvestable after the seedpods mature. For fresh use, pick immature pods. Pods will continue to grow until the first frost. For dry uses, wait until the pods turn brown.

Companion Plants

Cowpeas release the chemical allelopathic, killing competing plants when they germinate, and crowd out other plants, so there are not many good plants to pair with them.

Fenugreek is a good choice, and it is an exciting herb used in Asian dishes. Other options would be summer blooming flower plants such as cosmos or coreopsis (tickseed). These flowers will attract pollinators benefiting the garden; cut flowers are always great sellers at most farmer's markets.

Uses

Cowpeas are useful. When young, the leaves are edible, like spinach. People enjoy raw, cooked, or pickled cowpeas.

Roasting green cowpeas with olive oil and kosher salt creates a healthy snack. Brewing cowpeas produces a coffee-like drink popular in the Middle East and parts of Asia.

Planting cowpeas into a food plot creates a salad bar for livestock or wild animals. Hay or silage production cowpeas provide protein.

Cowpeas have medical uses. Cowpeas are a great source of fiber that can help heart health by lowering cholesterol. Cowpeas can help reduce plaque in the blood vessels. Cowpeas are full of free radicals, making them great for detoxing.

Fun Facts

- Cowpeas are a natural source of tryptophan, making them a natural sleep aid.
- Cowpeas are an excellent source of iron.
- Cowpeas are the main ingredients in the traditional New Year Day dish Hoppin Johns.
- The Black Eyed Peas are an American musical group named after the most popular cowpea variety.
- Sailors ate pickled cowpeas leaves to prevent scurvy.
- Cowpeas are sometimes called goatpeas.
- Cowpeas were originally called *mogette* (French for nun). The black eye in the center of the bean (where it attaches to the pod) reminded people of a nun's head attire.
- 2017 was the year of the cowpea in Missouri.

Selected Varieties

Black Eye or purple hull pea is the most popular of the cowpeas. The seeds are white with a black eye around the hilum. It is a loosely packed seed with the classic kidney shape. If gardening or selling produce in the south, this is a must-have.

Big Red Ripper is an Arkansas heirloom that also goes by the name Mandy and Tory. It is a highly productive (producing 18 seeds per pod) vine variety growing up to 8 feet long. This a day-length sensitive plant slowing production as the days get shorter.

Blue Goose peas are a highly productive heirloom from the 1880s that grows 36 inches tall. These peas can produce as many as 20 seeds per pod. This first-class tasting cowpea has a captivating blue/grey color combination.

Botswana Black-Eyed Pea is a deep-rooted African heirloom. It is one of the first varieties to make it to the Americas in the 1600s during the slave trade. This traditional pea is easy to grow and is very hardy, but it produces a tiny seed. However, there is a benefit to this smaller size because it stores and cooks easier when dried. This pea's body has a whiter body and darker eye than most other varieties giving this pea a more striking appearance.

Brown Eyed Peas are an heirloom that comes in different colors. This cowpea can produce pods that vary in color from lavender to green—cooking any variety of this cowpea turns it brown. The best word to describe this cowpea is charismatic.

Crowder Peas are a heavy producing black speckled heirloom. The seeds are "crowded" in the pod, which explains its name. It is a globular-shaped pea. The heavy production of this cowpea makes it an excellent investment.

Clay Pea is a rare southern heirloom from the Civil War era. This rare cowpea makes it a perfect choice for growers wanting to specialize in rare vegetables. It also goes by the name iron pea because of its color.

Green-Eyed Pea is a very rare heirloom from Missouri. During the 1880s, this pea was famous because of the large size. This cowpea lost favor because people preferred the look of the black-eyed pea—a great item to grow and market to the farm to table or sustainability crowd.

Holstein Cowpea is an heirloom patterned like a Holstein cow. It is a bush-style cowpea that thrives in southern states. For market growers, this is a great variety because it is a productive cowpea with interesting markings.

Lady Cream Peas or cream peas are a loose pod cowpea. The lady cream pea produces a good number of seeds per pod.

These white peas have no additional color and, when cooked, they create a clear pot of liquid. It is sweet-tasting with a creamy texture, making it great for soups.

Purple Hull Speckled Peas or Old Timers Pea is a speckled version of the black-eyed pea. The main difference is this pea's speckling. With the industrialization and standardization of food manufacturing, these cowpeas lost to cleaner-looking black-eyed peas. Today's emphasis on locally grown food and sustainability makes this item a prime candidate for a triumphed return.

Rice Pea is the smallest of all cowpeas. These white peas are slightly larger than rice and are easy to cook; when dry, it cooks in just 40 minutes! The small bushes that produce this cowpea are very productive. This pea was popular pre-Civil War.

White Acre Peas are kidney-shaped cowpeas with a blunt end. This cowpea pod is semi-crowded with tiny tan seeds. The real place-sounding name of this cowpea makes it a candidate for branding purposes. These cowpeas taste best when cooked with butter, bacon, or both. They pair quite nicely with cornbread and greens. This variety is excellent for farm-to-table restaurants.

Whippoorwill Cowpea is an heirloom grown by Thomas Jefferson at Monticello. It was the standard in the south during the early 1880s. When grown in fertile soil, it will produce 6-feet long runners! If grown in poor soil conditions, it will grow as a bush. This variety comes in either a white or a speckled version. Both versions are productive and great tasting.

Cucumbers

"Heaven is a homegrown cucumber" ~ **Alys Fowler**

Cucumbers teach people to be in control of their emotions.
The inside of a cucumber can be 20 degrees cooler than the
air around the outside. Just as hot temperatures cause
produce to rot, *hot heads cause souls to rot*.

Being as cool as a cumber has four benefits. First, rational
thinking is better than irrational responses. Second, a cool
head makes assessments more accurate. Cool, calm, and
collected people can better separate problems from
symptoms than hot-headed people. Third, proper planning
is a must. Fourth, being calm leads to better plan execution.
The advice being cool as a cucumber is as relevant today as
it was when Samuel Pepys coined this phrase in the 1700s.

Cucumbers are tropical vegetables growing as either a bush
or vine. They grow well in warm weather conditions with a
"lightweight," fertile soil. Cucumbers are members of the
gourd family.

History

Cucumbers had a modest beginning in the foothills of the
Himalayan Mountains. This humble vegetable made its way
to Egypt around 2,000 BC. From Egypt, it spread through
Africa.

Trading with Greece gave cucumbers voyage across the Mediterranean Sea. The Roman conquest of Greece allowed the cucumber to expand its influence into Europe and Asia.

Cucumber pickling began in Mesopotamia around 2,000 BC. Pickling gave cucumbers an advantage over its competitors. Pickling also helped people travel further and gave food to armies as they expanded and conquered other nations.

Pickles help build the Roman Empire. The Romans fed cucumbers to soldiers because they thought they made soldiers stronger and increased their spiritual strength. Pickles helped Europe through the Dark Ages and fed explorers during the Age of Discovery.

Competitive Advantage

Cucumbers are highly productive, and it makes sense to grow high output items. Also, cucumber plants replace picked fruit until the first frost.

To differentiate yourself from competitors, focus on unique varieties. Many people grow the same type of cucumber. To stand out, seek out various combinations and compelling stories to go with them.

Pickling cucumbers is one of the best things to do with a cucumber. Pickles are a fun item to market. Pickling cucumbers ensure hard work is profitable. Pickles are popular and local farms need to develop a niche in this market. Many specialty pickle products have come to grocery stores and catalogs in recent years. There is no reason that small-batch pickle products should not be at your market booth.

Marketing and Sales Strategies

Cucumbers are popular in salads, sandwiches, and as pickles. Cucumbers can be either slicing or pickling with a few dual variety options. The type of cucumber will guide your marketing message. Cucumbers are an excellent item for cross-promoting with other products such as lettuce, tomatoes, or any other salad add-in.

Cucumbers are a great candidate for a value-added product. The most apparent value-added product is pickles. Cucumber sauce is an often-overlooked condiment that can be another value-added product for growers. Bottling cucumber sauce makes for a unique item seldom seen in most farmer's markets. In addition to pickles, premade salads with cucumber toppings could be a great product. Cucumber water is a trendy drink that may be another good seller in the right market.

Promoting cucumber's health benefits will help move products. Remind customers that cucumbers are a healthy snack and something fun to add to their lunch.

Prepackaging cucumbers with your farm logo gives customers something they can easily handle. It will improve sales and speed up transaction times. The packaging needs to communicate cucumbers are super healthy and tasty. Packaging helps create brand loyalty, and well-designed packaging communicates quality.

Production and growing

- **Soil and pH** - Cucumbers need well-drained loose soil. The optimal pH is between 6.0 and 7.0.
- **Nutrients** - Cucumbers need nitrogen (N). Too little nitrogen will produce pinched-looking fruits. Phosphorus (P) is essential, especially for flower and fruit production. If the soil pH is slightly above or below neutral, phosphorus becomes extremely important. Calcium (Ca) is essential; without it, flowers can fall off, the fruit may not mature, and they will be tasteless if they do.
- **Water** - Cucumbers require consistent watering. For optimal results, water the equivalent of one inch of water each week - slightly more when temps reach over 90 degrees and even more when temperatures are over 100 degrees. Inconsistent or insufficient watering leads to bitter-tasting and small fruit.
- **Spacing** - Cucumbers need trellising 8 to 12 inches apart in beds with the plants outlining the bed. In rows, hills with one or two seedlings should be spaced about 3-feet

apart, with rows 4 to 5-feet apart. Space bush varieties 3-feet apart in all directions.

- **Growing Temp** - Cucumbers germinate when the soil temperature is between 60 - 90 degrees.
- **Pests** - The most notable cucumber pests are aphids, cucumber beetles, whiteflies, and thrips. Cucumber beetles are either striped or spotted and will devour seedlings, leaves, and blossoms. Whiteflies feed on leaves' underside, drinking the plant's sap, thus robbing the plant of nutrients needed for survival.
- **Disease** - Common cucumber diseases include powdery mildew and downy mildew. Various viral diseases can consist of the cucumber mosaic virus, squash mosaic virus, watermelon mosaic virus, and zucchini yellow mosaic virus.
- **Hardiness Zones** - Cucumbers grow best in Zones 4 - 11.
- **Tips** - Vined cucumbers need a sturdy trellis in full sunlight. Cucumbers are some of the easiest plants to grow. All they need is reasonably fertile soil with a steady supply of water.
- **Harvest** – The variety determines harvest size – the bigger the cucumber, the harder the skin, and the more bitter the taste. As a general rule of thumb, slicing cucumbers grow to about 6 or 8 inches in length, while the pickling cucumbers are shorter (3 to 4 inches). Pick cucumbers daily as they are prolific.

Companion Plants

Plant cucumber in beds with greens, spinach, or lettuce under the trellis. It will give these plants a longer growing period and the producer more income. Cucumbers do well with radishes, broccoli, beans, peas, and cauliflower. Corn and sunflowers are natural cucumber trellises.

Potatoes and cucumbers need separation. Cucumbers will also cross-pollinate with most melons and will compete with these plants for resources. Melons and cucumber also attract the same pests making any attack more devastating.

Uses

Snacks, salads, and condiments are popular cucumber uses. **Cucumbers are much more than great food.** Cucumbers are popular skincare items. For thousands of years, people have used cucumbers to moisturize dry eyes, make facial masks, and tone skin. Cucumbers can treat sunburns and provide a natural energy boost. Cucumbers can even clean and shine things up.

Cucumbers are high in fiber and can reduce constipation and lower cholesterol. They are sources of potassium and aid in sodium management, and they inhibit inflammatory enzymes. Cucumbers contain polyphenols or lignans, which are cancer preventers. Also, cucumbers contain phytonutrients called cucurbitacins, which have anti-cancer properties.

Fun Facts

- Cucumbers are the 4th most cultivated vegetable in the world.
- Cucumbers are 90% water.
- Cucumbers can be 20 degrees cooler on the inside than the ambient temperature.
- Cucumbers can eliminate bacteria that cause bad breath.
- Cucumbers can eliminate toxins in the body and can help reduce hangovers.
- People eat on average 9 pounds of cucumbers each year.
- Cleopatra claimed cucumbers made her beautiful.
- Dill pickles out sell sweet pickles by 2 to 1.
- Pickle juice popsicles are popular in many parts of the south, and the fast-food restaurant Sonic has even sold pickle juice slushes.
- Columbus grew pickles in Haiti so that his crew would have something to eat and to prevent scurvy.
- Berrien Springs, Michigan, has dubbed itself the Christmas Pickle Capital of the World.
- Amerigo Vespucci was a well-known pickle-merchant.
- Shakespeare brought cucumber idioms into mainstream use by creating the phrase, "You are in a pickle."

Selected Varieties

Ancash Market is a Peruvian heirloom from the early 1500s. Seed companies market it under the names Pepino Criollo Chacasino or Ancashino. It grows well in most parts of North America; it is pest and mildew-resistant. The fruits of this cucumber are best when picked at 6-inches.

African Horned Cucumber is a fun heirloom from Africa. This cucumber has a prickly exterior that turns orange when ripe. The fruit of this cucumber looks like green jelly with membranes. This seedy fruit is sweet-tasting and is a good conversation starter.

Aonaga Jibai is a sweet and tender Japanese heirloom. It is a vigorous cucumber that produces 8-inch long fruit with unassuming seeds. Tanaka & Co. introduced this variety to America in 1939. It is drought and disease-resistant and is an excellent choice for novice growers that want wanting

Armenian Cucumber is a light green heirloom that has a mild taste. It is a good grower of uniform fruits that reach 24 inches in length! This cucumber tastes best when it is 18-inches long. It is a slicing cucumber.

Boston Pickling Cucumber is an old-time favorite dating back to the mid-19th century. A very popular dual-purpose cucumber that tastes great either as a pickle or sliced on a salad. This variety is straightforward to raise, prolific, and fashionable. Always a steadfast seller.

Chicago Pickling Cucumber is a North American heirloom designed for northern growers. This great pickling cucumber goes well sliced on sandwiches or salads. It is a thin skin cucumber that allows for greater soaking of pickle solution. This cucumber has been popular since its release in 1888. It is pest and disease-resistant that produces until the first frost.

Chinese Yellow Cucumber is an heirloom of a different color. This cucumber lost out in marketing because of its yellow color. Behind its yellow exterior is a great tasting fruit. This fruit can grow up to 10-inches long while remaining crisp and mild. This cucumber is great sliced or pickled and needs consideration. The key to selling this cucumber is to provide customer samples.

Crystal Apple Cucumber is a Chinese heirloom. It is an Australian favorite that looks like an apple. It is easy to eat raw because of its thin-skin. This cumber's thin skin makes it perfect for pickling and experimenting with various flavorings.

Delikatesse Cucumber is a German heirloom. It is a pickling cucumber when small and a slicing variety when long. These fruits are small, light green with stipples. A great-looking cucumber best marketed as a non-GMO variety. Very prolific.

Double Yield Cucumber was introduced in the early 1900s by the Harris Seed Company who claimed that it would produce 2 or 3 cucumbers for every cucumber harvested. This cucumber consistently makes crisp, off the vine cucumbers — one of the highest producing heirlooms available.

Dragon's Egg Cucumber is a beautiful heirloom from Croatia that looks like a light green egg growing on a vine. The name of this cucumber makes a great conversation starter at any produce stand. Pickling this cucumber gives a great subtitle to any brand name. This cucumber is sure to be gobbled up by Harry Potter fans, *How to Train Your Dragon* and other fans of mythical creatures and stories.

Early Fortune Cucumber is an heirloom variety from the early 1900s. It also goes by the name dark pickler, even though it is popular for slicing. It is dependable and produces more quickly than other types. It is a great salad add-in or as the main feature for a bacon cucumber sandwich when picked at 6 to 8 inches long.

Fin De Meaux is a French heirloom that is short and spiny. It is easy to grow and makes a great addition to any garden. This cucumber will turn bitter and harsh if not picked young and petite (2-inches or under is best). When harvested at the optimal time, the Fin De Meaux gives cornichons a nice buttery flavor.

Gagon Cucumber is an interesting heirloom from Bhutan. This cucumber does well in most areas in North America. It tolerates cooler climates as well as the heat and humidity of the south. In Bhutan, this is a cooking cucumber, but it does well sliced or when pickled. This cucumber can reach 20-inches in length. A flamboyant character available in red or purple colors.

Gele Tros is a Dutch heirloom. This cucumber came to the Netherlands as the Germanic people fled from the Romans. This sunshine yellow cucumber is fascinating looking and tastes excellent when picked. A workhorse of a cucumber that delivers hefty yields until frost, it is rare even in its home country.

Hmong Cucumber is an heirloom from Southeast Asia. It is one of the eldest cucumbers currently available. Easy to grow and very prolific, this cucumber is popular in Asian markets. This cucumber, unlike other varieties, stays mild in taste as it matures.

Japanese Long Cucumber is an heirloom variety carried over from the Han Dynasty. This cucumber is a burpless cucumber that grows up to 20 inches long without becoming bitter. This cucumber is excellent for pickling or salads. The size of the cucumber is a spectacle. This cucumber is perfect for farmers markets and roadside stands.

Jaune Dickfleischige Cucumber is a French or German heirloom, depending on the source. This cucumber is a centerpiece of cucumber history. It produces a green fruit that turns yellow and can grow to five pounds without turning bitter while remaining crisp. This cucumber deserves consideration for any market garden. It is a heavy producer of a deliciously wonderful cucumber.

Khiva Cucumber is a rare French heirloom that looks much like a kiwi fruit or a small-netted melon. Initially, it was sold as a Russian heirloom as a way to generate interest. This plant produces short and thick fruits that are 4 to 6 inches in length. This Khiva vine is long and trailing. This cooking cucumber is popular in stir-fry and can be sliced or pickled, making it a triple-use cucumber.

Kish White Cucumber is an Amish heirloom from the Kishacoquillas Valley region of the Appalachian Mountains in Pennsylvania. The Kish White is a white pickling cucumber with creamy yellow skin. This very productive and vigorous cucumber produces curious-looking pickles that sell fast.

Lemon Cuke Cucumber looks like a lemon but tastes like a cucumber. It was first fraudulently marketed as a lemon substitute, which killed its reputation. It is an excellent choice for cucumber water or other cucumber drink. This cucumber is a good grower and has above average in cucurbitacin, the chemical that causes bitterness in cucumbers.

Metki Dark Green Serpent is an Armenian heirloom from the 1400s. When small, it is an excellent pickler, but when large, it is a great slicer. It is one of the longer cucumbers reaching lengths of 3-feet. A very rare and prolific cucumber that growers should consider for the market. Some seed companies marketed this as a melon. It will provide a unique item for any product mix.

Mexican Sour Gherkin Cucumber a Mexican heirloom that looks like tiny melons. This cucumber makes a great item to market as pickled melons. This plant is very productive, and the fruit is a great conversation starter. This cucumber is the perfect size for a snack.

Natsu Fushinari Cucumber is a Japanese heirloom that is very disease resistant. It produces an outstanding tasting pale green fruit. This highly productive cucumber has fruit at virtually every node. These cucumbers grow to be up 8 inches long without bitterness; it does not do well on a trellis!

Parisian Pickling Cucumber is an old French heirloom that made its way to America just before 1900. This pickling cucumber is a perfect cornichon. A rare cucumber on the rebound would be an excellent cucumber to grow to create a value-added pickle product for any grower with a farm store.

Richmond Green Apple is an heirloom Australia. Legend has it that this is the forerunner to the lemon cuke cucumber. A creative and enterprising salesperson selectively bred this cucumber to eliminate stripes, making it look more like a lemon. This cucumber is typically mild tasting, juicy, and sweet. The cucumber is best raw, but it may be pickled.

Sagami Hanjiro Cucumber is a traditional cucumber from the Sagami area of Japan. This two-toned cucumber is perfect for slicing. Very popular in Japan, this cucumber is rare in North America. It should do well at farmers markets, farm stores, and roadside stands. This cucumber is not as seedy as other varieties.

Sikkim Cucumber is an old heirloom from the Himalayas. It is a cooking cucumber that is popular in many Indian and Asian dishes. It is rare in North America, popular with Asian or Indian natives or followers of their traditional cuisine. This cucumber is red, making it unique and attractive.

Suyo Long Cucumber is a Chinese heirloom that can reach 18 inches and still be bitter-free. This burpless cucumber is perfect for slicing and using on salads, sandwiches, or by itself. This long curly green cucumber is visually appealing and easy to grow. Its heat tolerance makes it perfect for the south. For straight fruit, grow on a trellis, and for curvy fruit, grow on the ground. I prefer a mixture of straight and curly fruit.

White Emerald Cucumber is an heirloom from Thailand and is a popular cumber for chefs and food lovers. This cucumber is very adaptable and is suited for any cucumber-growing region. The fruit is seedy and green, and the skin is light green, almost white. This cucumber requires very little care other than trellising and harvesting.

Garlic

"Garlic is divine. Few food items can taste so many distinct ways"
~**Anthony Bourdain**

Garlic is one of Mother Nature's purest joys and one of the Earth's best gifts. It is one of the oldest flavorings that brings out the best in meat, vegetables, and people. As hunting and gathering gave way to farming and animal domestication, garlic was there, making food enjoyable. Garlic transformed food from mere sustenance to a pleasurable experience.

Garlic allowed our ancestors to enjoy meals together; it caused humans to slow down and enjoy their meals. This extended mealtime gave rise to conversations. These conversations gave way to shared intelligence, meaning, stories, and the development of culture. Garlic allowed humans the resources necessary to prosper. Marcel Boulestin said it best when he said, *"It is not an exaggeration to say that peace and happiness begin, geographically, where garlic is used in cooking."* The proof of this is in the history books.

Garlic comes in three basic types -- hardneck, softneck, and greathead. Each one has unique characteristics.

- **Hardneck Garlic** is the garlic of choice for growers that want something other than the plain grocery store variety. Hardneck Garlic tends to have a more complex taste with heat ranging from mild to spicy. It is susceptible to soil and weather conditions allowing hardneck garlic to develop a regional flair. This garlic is an excellent choice for farm-to-table growers. It's a cold, hardy garlic that performs well in the north. A drawback for hardnecks is their lack of storability lasting only 3-4 months once cured.

- **Softneck Garlic** is the most popular grocery store garlic. This garlic provides a familiar and conversant product for customers. This garlic's soft neck allows for braiding, and braided garlic is easier to store and display. This type of garlic is smaller than hardneck garlic, but it has more cloves. Softneck garlic grows best in the south and stores well, lasting 12 months or more.

- **Great-headed** (Elephant) garlic is the least hardy of the garlic types. This leek relative has an onion flavor. The bulbs and cloves are quite large, with about 4-cloves to a bulb—a good item for creating an eye-catching display.

History

Garlic is one of agriculture's oldest crops. Garlic originated as a wild plant in central Asia. Early humans discovered the root of this plant added flavor to other foods. This taste enchantment resulted in migrating people carrying it as they explored the world.

Human migration brought garlic to the Egyptians and Indians over 5,000 years ago. From Egypt, it migrated to the Babylonians and Chinese. Garlic then spread to Africa, the Middle East, and Europe. Then from Europe, garlic made its way across the Atlantic to the New World.

The Spanish and Portuguese introduced garlic to Latin and South America. It would take another three centuries before North America embraced garlic. Today, garlic is a much sought-after product that adds taste to most any dish, and it is renowned for its health benefits.

Throughout its 5,000 years of recorded history, garlic has had little diversity in its available varieties. Unlike some heirlooms that boast numerous types, garlic has remained simple primarily because it is nearly perfect. Only in the last few hundred years have new varieties been developed.

Competitive Advantage

Garlic is widely grown for fresh market use by many producers on a small scale for local markets. In the United States, there are only a few large-scale producers for fresh sales. With the local food trend increasing and more people actively searching for locally grown products and garlic's price, it makes sense to produce it.

Growing garlic is a massive opportunity for people looking for a high-profit item that is in demand. During any given month, 44% of grocery store shoppers have purchased garlic. Also, grocery stores have reported eight years of garlic growth (2010 – 2018), and in 2016 garlic sales increased 12%.

Garlic is very prolific, producing up to 15,000 pounds per acre. Grocery stores routinely charge $2.00 per pound for the run-of-the-mill garlic, and specialty stores charge upwards of $5.00 a pound for garlic; the profit potential is enormous. Some direct-market growers sell bulbs for $1.00 or more depending on the variety and local market.

Marketing and Sales Strategies

Garlic is the only universally used seasoning. Garlic has both culinary and health appeal. It may reduce the risk of cancer, improve blood flow, and lower cholesterol. When selling garlic, focus the marketing message on its culinary and health uses.

Merchandising garlic is essential. The garlic display needs to be prominent and visible from a distance. Fill shallow bins, crates, or baskets slightly overfilling at an angle. The tilt of angle needs to be just enough to increase the line of sight without causing garlic to spill out.

These containers need to have your logo and information about the variety of garlic offered. In addition to the tilted boxes, place garlic next to the most popular garlic pairing. For example, tomatoes are always big sellers. Placing garlic next to paste tomatoes with recipes for pasta sauce will encourage people to buy garlic and tomatoes.

Good-looking garlic is a great seller. When selling raw garlic, sell only the best quality, clean, and disease-free garlic. Use the less desirable garlic for value-added products such as powder, garlic salt, pasta sauce, breads, etc.

Only cleaned and cured garlic needs to be at the market. Perfectly trimmed garlic in tightly wrapped bulbs is what most people are looking for when they buy garlic. *Braiding garlic is a great strategy to move garlic.* Braided garlic is attractive and easy to handle. Also, braided garlic allows for various price points depending on the size of the braid.

Educate customers about the superiority of raw garlic. It is heartbreaking that the only experience many people have had with garlic is in its powder form. Offer a free sample to people that have never experienced garlic. It is a great way to make a connection and to build future business. Build a bond with your customers by talking with and educating them on garlic. You will gain a long-time customer and a new friend.

Production and growing

- **Soil and pH** - Garlic does best in well-drained and fertile soils with lots of loose organic matter. Rocks and clays will create misshapen bulbs, so it is vital to remove as many stones as possible or grow in raised beds. The optimal pH range for garlic is 6.0 - 7.0.
- **Nutrients** - Garlic does best with continuous use of a high phosphorus (P) fertilizer such as a 10-10-10 or 15-30-15. The best time to add nitrogen (N) is during fall and before May 1st.
- **Water** - Garlic requires moist but not wet soil. The soil should be thoroughly soaked weekly to a depth of at least one inch. Sandy soils require more frequent watering. Watering needs to stop two weeks before harvest; otherwise, the bulbs will stain.
- **Spacing** – Plant garlic cloves in double rows at least 6 inches apart. Center the rows on beds, 30 inches apart. Plant cloves pointed side up, with the clove base two to three inches from the soil surface.
- **Growing Temp** - Hardneck garlic requires a cold period for sprouting. Growers in warmer climates should store garlic in a cool, dry place (45 - 50 degrees) for three weeks before planting. Hardneck garlic grows best in the north, and softneck garlic grows better in the south.
- **Pests** – Garlic, for the most part, is pest resistant. The onion maggot may be a problem. Onion maggots bore into plant stems, causing the plants to turn yellow and wilt.

- **Disease** - Garlic is vulnerable to different types of rot. Fusarium basal rot is the most common. Weed management and seed selection are the best courses of action to prevent this.
- **Hardiness Zones** - Softneck garlic grows best in zones 3 - 9. Hardneck garlic does best in zones 3 - 6.
- **Tips** – Plant garlic cloves a week or two after the first killing frost. Top the beds with three to four inches of leaf or straw mulch to prevent fluctuating temperatures during the winter and early spring. Also, this will control weeds.
- **Harvest** – Garlic variety and growing zones determine when to harvest garlic. June and July is garlic harvesting season. Harvest when the lower leaves turn brown and when half or slightly more than half of the upper leaves are green. Harvest garlic plants with shoots and bulbs attached. Knock off any large clumps of soil. Place garlic in a warm, dry, airy place for three to four weeks to cure. The goal is to dry the sheaths surrounding the bulbs. After curing, cut the shoots one-half to one inch above the bulbs, and the roots trimmed close to the bulb base.

Companion Plants

Garlic does well with most other plants. Garlic is beneficial to many other plants because it is an outstanding pest repellant. Garlic is good for the soil and feeds soil microbes. Garlic pairs with cabbage and protects cabbage from cabbageworms and diamondback months.

Other plants that do well next to garlic are peppers, tomatoes, and lettuce. When companion planting with garlic, the most important thing to consider is the harvest timing of the involved plants.

Though few, some plants suffer when planted near garlic. Do not plant garlic next to asparagus, peas, beans, sage, or parsley. These plants will not hurt garlic, but garlic will hurt these plants and limit their production.

Uses

Garlic's primary purpose is as an ingredient or seasoning. All parts are useable, but the bulb is what most people use. Use garlic stems the same way you use chives. Garlic cloves may be consumed raw, roasted, sautéed, or dried.

Garlic, when used for skincare, can tighten and exfoliate the skin. It needs mixing with finely minced garlic, olive oil, facial cleanser, and sugar. Also, adding a few garlic cloves to a warm footbath makes it antifungal.

In addition to food and skincare, garlic has many health benefits. For example, garlic improves heart health, lowers high blood pressure, and reduces cholesterol and coronary heart disease.

Fun Facts

- Garlic has adhesive properties.

- Egyptian builders ate garlic because they believe it gave them strength.
- Garlic keeps evil spirits and vampires away.
- Garlic comes in more than 450 varieties.
- Garlic can grow up to 4 feet tall.
- Garlic is an excellent source of trace minerals, including iron, magnesium, zinc, and selenium.
- Garlic is a good source of Vitamin B and C and contains various amino acids.
- Garlic is toxic to dogs and cats.
- Garlic is known as Russian penicillin.
- Garlic is a blood thinner.
- The fear of garlic is known as alliumphobia.
- California leads in garlic production with 90% of the garlic grown in the United States.
- China leads the world in garlic production.
- National garlic day is April 19th.
- Deepak Sharma holds the world record for eating garlic with 34 cloves in a minute.
- The longest garlic bread was 54 feet and 10 inches long.
- The longest garlic braid was 836 feet long.
- There are dozens of garlic festivals, including the Gilroy Garlic Festival, one of America's largest food festivals.
- A single 10-foot row of garlic will produce up to 5 pounds of garlic.
- Hardneck garlic will grow by multiples of 400-600%. Softneck garlic grows by multiples of 600-1000%.

Selected Varieties

Applegate Garlic is a softneck garlic that produces large bulbs. This garlic makes multiple layers of consistently sized cloves. The Applegate garlic produces up to 18 cloves per bulb. The cloves have a snug papery covering that is a soft yellow to white with some purple-hued patches. The cloves are off-white and have a mild, creamy flavor without the hot, intense finish of other garlic varieties.

Asian Tempest Garlic is a hardneck garlic from South Korea that produces small bulbs just two inches in diameter. This bulb divides into 5 to 7 cloves that are crescent-shaped. The bulb wrappers or skin is firm with purple streaks. When eaten raw, this garlic is hot, but when cooked, its hotness becomes sweet.

Bogatyr Marbled Purple Stripe Garlic is a hardneck variety from Russia. This garlic is intensely hot when raw. The flavor turns sharp when it is chopped, minced, or pureed. The Bogatyr can also be roasted or sautéed. In Russia and Western Europe, this garlic is typically roasted and added to soups. This garlic pairs well with cream-based sauces, olive oils, pasta, grilled steak, seafood, and other roasted proteins. This garlic has above average storability with storage upwards of 10 months.

Chesnok Red Garlic is a hardneck heirloom from the Republic of Georgia. This purple striped garlic has a medium-hot flavor that sustains its flavor when cooked. The bulbs of the Chesnok average 8 to 20 cloves, making it a larger garlic type. The cloves of this garlic are longer and thinner than other kinds of garlic. This garlic routinely wins awards at garlic festivals and won the best garlic by *Sunset Magazine.* When properly dried, this garlic has above-average storability.

Chinese Garlic is an heirloom hardneck from Asia that performs best roasted, sautéed, or baked. The Chinese garlic has good heat and an intense flavor. It is the quintessential garlic for traditional Chinese cuisine because it pairs well with bold flavors, spicy ingredients, and rich foods. It is also a great complement to conventional Chinese spices such as chilies, ginger, and soy sauce. The Chinese garlic has moderate storability and will keep up to five months when properly dried and stored in a cool, dry place.

Elephant Garlic is not really a garlic, but a leek used like garlic. Originally from China, this is sold as garlic by seed catalogs and retailers, explaining its inclusion. This softball-size bulb produces 5 to 7 cloves per bulb. It has a milder taste than garlic, so people who cannot tolerate garlic but like garlic flavor can use this. When sautéed, the crushed cloves caramelize much better than traditional garlic. Elephant garlic is an allicin source (allicin reduces inflammation).

German Red Garlic is large hardneck garlic that can produce up to 15 cloves per bulb. When planted in the spring, this garlic can be harvested in just 90 days, making it a mid-season variety. German Red is full-bodied with a strong and spicy taste. This white garlic produces purple heads. The cloves are easy to peel and are a joy for cooking. This garlic has a robust, classic flavor that is spicy and delicious – very popular with chefs and foodies. This garlic does exceptionally well in cooler climates. It arrived in America over a century ago with German immigrants.

Inchelium Red Garlic is a softneck heirloom discovered growing on an Indian reservation. It is mild at harvest. The flavor rallies as it ages with just a touch of heat at its peak flavor. Larger than average, it grows up to 3 inches in diameter and produces up to 12 cloves. When dried and stored correctly, it can up to 10 months. This garlic does best when planted in the fall for the following season. It is one of the easier types to grow; however, its size means it takes longer to cure.

Italian Garlic is a hardneck heirloom that has many different sub-varieties. As the name suggests, it is perfect for Italian foods, braiding, roasting, and raw use. A good strategy for garlic growers is to plant multiple members of this family. It will provide a great assortment of rich and colorful products for the market. They are massive, producing 8 - 12 cloves per bulb.

Kashmiri Garlic is a single clove heirloom from the Himalayas. It also goes by the name Himalayan garlic or snow garlic because it grows in the snow in high altitudes. Some growers have had success with it in America, especially growers that live in the mountains.

It is extremely rare and has a cult following. Successful growers find they have a loyal customer base. Kashmiri garlic has a rugged, golden-brown husk with a rounded flat side that transforms into a point. People use Kashmiri garlic raw and cooked.

Kettle River Giant Garlic is a hardneck heirloom from the Pacific Northwest. One of the largest varieties with bulbs that reach 4 inches across. This hardneck has the storing longevity of a softneck but with the classic flavor of a hardneck. It is a good shipping garlic - perfect for online sales.

Korean Garlic is a vigorous hardneck heirloom that can take the heat. It has dark green foliage with a strong hot and spicy flavor.

Merrifield Rocambole Garlic is a purple hardneck garlic that produces large bulbs and double cloves. It is cool weather garlic does better in northern states. The wrappings of this garlic are light brown with purple streaks. This great-tasting garlic has a classic flavor. The bulb of this garlic produces 7 - 10 cloves per bulb.

Music Garlic is an Italian hardneck heirloom with a hot flavor when raw and a sweet taste when cooked. Perfect for the cooler climates of the north. It is trendy in Canada.

This small bulb averages 5 to 7 cloves per bulb. Music Garlic is an outstanding producer and can grow up to 13,500 pounds per acre. Also, it can be stored for up to a year under proper conditions. It is an excellent variety for direct marketers and growers selling online.

Persian Star Garlic is a hardneck heirloom from Uzbekistan. This attractive garlic has purple streaks, flavorful, and nutty when cooked or roasted. It is stunning and displays well. The cloves of this garlic look like an eight-point star. Persian Star Garlic is a unique choice to grow and always a good seller.

Polish Mid-Season Garlic is a softneck heirloom that immigrated to America with Polish immigrants in the early 1900s. It is an excellent option for traditional Polish cuisine, such as Polish sausage. This hot garlic stays hot even after roasting. The heat and the classic taste are a spicy food complement. It is easy to grow and does find just about anywhere.

Romanian Red Garlic is a hardneck heirloom that has large bulbs with large cloves. It is a classic western European variety that does excellent with traditional European fare. When eaten raw, this garlic has a strong garlic flavor with mild heat. When cooked or roasted, the flavor turns nutty. The Romanian Red has good storability, and each bulb can produce 4 to 5 cloves. Many growers report this addictive garlic has repeat customers asking for it by name.

Siberian Garlic is a hardneck heirloom that does better in the north. The Siberian garlic produces attractive bulbs that are light pink and can turn almost purple if grown in high iron soil. It is a resilient tasting garlic with just a hint of heat. The Siberian garlic has decent storability, though the heat reduces as it is stored, and it is one of the most productive types. It returns 80 pounds for every 10 pounds planted!

Silverskin Garlic is a softneck heirloom with beautiful, large bulbs. Sometimes this is called grocery store garlic because this what grocery stores carry. This garlic is widespread because of its high yields, storability, and shipping ease. It can be grown just about anywhere under any conditions. The tradeoff for this highly productive garlic is taste; it lacks other varieties' taste complexities and depth.

Spanish Roja Rocambole Garlic is a hardneck heirloom producing medium-sized bulbs. This garlic made its appearance in America around the 1900s when it arrived in Oregon. This garlic does fine in southern states. Sometimes marketed as Greek Garlic or Greek Blue Garlic, it does well in Spanish or Greek fares. It has moderate storability storing up to 6 months. This garlic has a classic garlic taste with easy-peel cloves.

Western Rose Garlic is a softneck heirloom. It is a sizeable late-season garlic easily stored with a year-long shelf life. For market sellers, this variety is an excellent braiding variety with a sharp taste.

Transylvanian Garlic is a softneck heirloom that has great marketing appeal. For fun, market this garlic as a vampire or evil spirit repellant by referencing its origin and making an instant Halloween seller.

The productive Transylvanian garlic has a classic garlic taste and produces up to 16 cloves per bulb. It is also easy to grow. This garlic has won best baking in garlic festivals throughout America.

Vostani Porcelain Garlic is a Siberian hardneck heirloom. The word vostani means to *rise up* and is an appropriate name for this garlic as it can grow taller than most other varieties. It is tasty. The Vostani is tiny and only produces four cloves per bulb. It does store well. Many growers report this garlic practically grows itself; it's attractive and packs good heat.

Greens (including collards)

*"The best comfort food will always be greens, cornbread, and fried chicken." ~ **Maya Angelou***

Greens are a source of comfort. They bring back memories; people associate greens with beloved family members, holidays, bygone days, and ancestral roots.

Greens are popular for many reasons. It could be the color because green symbolizes growth, nature, and rebirth. It could be the taste as greens taste like the good old days. Many people claim greens taste like grandmother's love and affection, the flavor of comfort and security.

It could be the smell of greens cooking. Food smells bring to life detailed and powerful memories. The scent of greens reminds people of time spent in the kitchen with parents or grandparents. The smell of greens may remind people of the time spent in the garden. The scent of greens reminds people of family and of what is vital.

Greens are biennials grown as annuals. Greens are fast harvesting, being ready in only 70 days. When harvesting the leaves, work from the bottom up so that the lower stem will be bare, making the plant look tree-like.

Fresh leaves grow from the center through cool weather. Harvest leaves when they are up to 10 inches long, dark green, and still young. Old leaves become tough or stringy.

Southern people hold collards and greens in high esteem; northern people are learning more about this delicacy. Greens and collards make great salads, but most people prefer cooking them. A quick search for greens and collards recipes will yield many ways to enjoy these items.

History

Greens predate human history. The greens of today originated in Asia from wild cabbage. The Greeks enjoyed greens and found that their resistance to frost provided a stable food source. After the Greeks, the Romans raised greens, and they spread throughout Europe as the Roman Empire spread.

In America, greens and collards provided food for slaves during the winter. Greens were cheap and easy to grow. As the freed slaves moved off plantations, they carried collards and greens with them. For years, this economic and social stigma hurt collard's mainstream popularity. However, in the past few decades, collards and green have been appearing in upscale southern restaurants. Today, people from all economic levels and social settings are embracing collards.

The rise of their popularity has been a source of controversy. There are "collard traditionalists" who call this spiritual food gentrification. Other people embrace its rise in popularity as a valuable tool in fighting the obesity epidemic.

I believe the increase in popularity is a good thing. This increased popularity will help save heirlooms from going extinct while educating people on the culture and heritage of an essential group of people from our nation's history. There is no reason that these opposing viewpoints cannot coexist.

Competitive Advantage

According to the USDA, greens and collards account for $200 million in sales (2017). Grocery stores report green sales are increasing at 3.2% per year. This modest growth and volume of sales is an excellent opportunity for local growers of heirloom products.

Greens and collards may be grown year-round with the help of hoop or greenhouses. Hydroponic systems allow for the mass production of greens and collards. Using modern technology to produce an heirloom crop allows the steady supply of a popular product for year-round cash flow.

Water and fertilizer automation makes growing more manageable, allowing you to deploy efforts into more labor-intensive areas. This year-round production allows for cash that gives producers the advantage of not having an off-farm job, allowing more time to focus on the farming enterprise.

Marketing and Sales Strategies

When marketing greens and collards, focus on the many ways to cook these items. A quick internet search will yield thousands of ideas and recipes. Use this research to create a top 10 list. This list should have a few standard recipes, a few simple, a few complicated, and a few local favorites. This list is handy to have at your stand or to pass along to customers.

In Raleigh, North Carolina, the State Farmers Market holds a "Colossal Collard Greens Day" just before Thanksgiving. There is no reason other people or markets cannot create a similar event. People like events and product-based events moves product.

Collards and greens are must-haves for Thanksgiving and New Year Days celebrations. Be sure to market black-eyed peas with collards for better cross-merchandising.

Production and growing

- **Soil and pH** - Collards do best in soil with lots of organic material that drains well. The optimum pH for collards is 6.0 to 7.5.
- **Nutrients** – Collards and greens require high nitrogen (N) and high potassium (K).
- **Water** - Collards need a lot of water in the first four weeks – at least the equivalent of an inch per week and medium water as it matures.

- **Spacing** - If growing in rows, collards should be 12 to 18 inches apart with rows at least 24 inches apart. If growing in beds, collards should be 12 inches apart in all directions.
- **Growing Temp** - Collards grow best when temperatures are between 60 to 65 degrees. Collards tolerate 70-degree temperatures but will bolt when temperatures are above 80 degrees for several days.
- **Pests** - Collards tend not to have many pest problems because it is a cool weather plant.
- **Disease** - Clubroot is common when the pH is low. Blackleg, a soil bacterium, is harmful to collards. Downy mildew is a fungal disease that can be problematic.
- **Hardiness Zones** - Collards are a national plant and grown in all hardiness zones in North America.
- **Tips** – Start collards 3 to 6 weeks before the final frost. Collards can handle a few light touches of frost but do not do well with a heavy frost or multiple frosts during a short period since collards are heavy feeders requiring a steady supply of fertilizer.
- **Harvest** – This depends upon the use and local selling requirements. If selling at a local market, regulations may require that the plant leaves and plant be intact. When this is the case, harvest when the leaves are 8 to 10 inches. If local regulations allow for bagging, harvest the leaves from the plant's bottom so the plant looks tree-like. It will encourage new growth.

Companion Plants

Greens and collards play well with the following plants: beets, bush beans, celery, cucumber, dill, garlic, geraniums, marigolds, onions, potatoes, and most herbs such as rosemary, sage, thyme, and mint.

Greens and collards do not play well with the following plants: grapes, Mexican marigolds, pole beans, rue, strawberries, and tomatoes. Most of the plants compete for resources except for strawberries which crowd out other plants.

Uses

Greens and collards are primary used as a side dish. Quiches and soups are great uses for collards, helping to turn a side dish into a main attraction. Both are a fun substitute for spinach; they are a superfood full of vitamins and minerals. Greens and Collards are a great source of Vitamin K, keeping bones strong. Both also bind to bad fat, helping reduce bad cholesterol.

Greens and collard greens are high in fiber. Both are useful in the management of diabetes, primarily type II diabetes. According to WebMD, Collard greens contain an antioxidant known as alpha-lipoic acid, which reduces glucose levels, increases insulin sensitivity, and prevents oxidative stress-induced damage.

Fun Facts

- Collard greens can grow 3 to 4 feet in height.
- Collard greens grow tiny edible yellow flowers arranged in pyramid-shaped clusters.
- Collard greens produce dry fruit that holds hundreds of tiny seeds in its second year.
- The name "collard" originates from the word "colewort," which translates into "wild cabbage."
- Non-heading cabbage or tree cabbage are other names for collards.
- Collard greens are a superfood and a great source of dietary fibers, vitamin B9, C, A, K; they include minerals such as iron, calcium, copper, manganese, and selenium.
- Collard greens are a low-calorie food that is a tasty part of a low-calorie diet. A 100 gram serving of collard greens contains only 30 calories.
- All parts of the collard plant are edible.
- Collards were grown by the Ancient Greeks.

Selected Varieties

Georgia Southern is an heirloom collard green that dates back to at least the Civil War period. Slaves grew this for food. This variety was popular because of its vigor. It is a heavy producer, and it tastes great. In southern Georgia, this plant can endure most winters.

Morris Heading Collard is an heirloom dating back to the 1800s. It was a classic variety popular in the south because it was slow to bolt, allowing more time to enjoy its incredible bounty.

Yellow Cabbage Collards is an heirloom from Asheville, North Carolina. In 1887, Colonel Branner observed yellow collard greens were tender and less bitter than other collards. He used this insight to develop a delicate, buttery green. These seeds, until recently, were only available to old-time southern seed savers—a great item to bring to market because of its years of selected breeding.

Vates Collards is a mid-Atlantic heirloom that is blue-green and is slow to bolt. This variety is both heat resistant and cold tolerant. It can grow two feet high and wide.

Champion Collard Greens is a good grower in the spring and early summer. This heirloom is often started outdoors just before the last frost. This variety has a good cabbage flavor that does excellent in soups, stews, and other cooked dishes. This variety makes an excellent add-in for coleslaw.

Kale

*"Eat kale sometimes, but skip it as a trend." ~ **Anna Getty***

Kale is intense, relentless, and loyal. I planted Russian kale one fall, and it grew tall and proud. The winter snow was no match for it, neither were the spring storms. I harvested leaves that would regrow. It was fierce, providing many meals.

Describing kale is like talking about a good friend. Kale is there when things are hard; it is there through the storms. Kale provides rebirth, rejuvenation, and restoration for a weary soul when the days get short.

Kale has substance. Fall kale reminds us that many of the greatest success stories start late. Like Ray Kroc, Colonel Sanders, Rodney Dangerfield, or Julia Child, who all made it big later in life. These people made it big when other people were slowing down and thinking about retirement.

Kale is an annual that takes 70 days to reach maturity. A hardy cool-season green is part of the cabbage family. Kale is unique enough to create its own story; it is a superfood that is super popular.

Kale grows best in the spring and fall and can tolerate fall frosts. When harvesting kale leaves, work from the bottom up so that the lower stem will be bare, making the plant look tree-like. Fresh leaves will continue to grow through cool weather.

History

The Greeks and Romans were the first users of kale. As western society expanded, kale expanded along with it. During the middle ages in Europe, kale spread with the crusades. And, during the period of exploration, settlers brought kale from Europe to the New World. In the 1600s, Russian traders brought kale to Canada.

Kale fell out of fashion after World War II. Kale is easy to grow, which made it widely available during the rationing of World War II when things like meat, dairy, and other products were not. It is why kale is considered one of WWII's unsung heroes.

The war ended, and people moved from the rural areas to the suburbs. Victory gardens disappeared, and people turned to grocery stores for food. Grocery stores carried what people wanted. People were tired of kale, so they did not buy it. Grocery stores stopped supplying it, and kale took a hiatus.

Kale is making a comeback. More people are embracing vegetable-based diets and are looking for healthier food options. Kale has a strong cult following, and the people who like kale really *like* kale.

Competitive Advantage

Kale is increasing in popularity. Kale tastes delicious; it is versatile and extremely healthy. There are many exciting versions of this plant that help producers differentiate. Kale, especially cold-hardy kale such as a Russian variety, provides a product that can produce year-round cash flow.

Marketing and Sales Strategies

Kale's prominence as a superfood needs to lead the marketing message. To take advantage of this, make kale appear as a lifestyle choice. Kale is a leading item in both the food trend world and the farm-to-table movement. Incorporate knowledge about both worlds into your discussions about kale with customers. It will appeal to your customer's emotional needs and will create brand loyalty.

Kale has many tag lines. People have used lines such as:

- Eat more kale
- Things go better with kale
- Kale is king
- Kale this
- Kale a superfood for a super living
- All about the kale life
- Kale powered
- Kale'd it
- Licensed to kale

These tag lines on a t-shirt with your farm name are a fantastic branding opportunity. Kale culture provides many fun options when it comes to marketing.

Kale can be marketed as a value-added flowering item. Flowering cabbage and kale offer an attractive complement to garden mum sales during the fall.

Production and growing

- **Soil and pH** - Kale prefers rich, loose soil with lots of organic material. The optimal pH for kale is between 5.5 and 6.5.
- **Nutrients** - Kale craves nitrogen (N). Kale needs phosphorus (P) as well as calcium (Ca). A 5-10-10 fertilizer or the organic equivalent is best for kale.
- **Water** - Kale needs a steady supply of water. The soil should be damp but not too wet - so drainage is essential. Kale may be grown hydroponically.
- **Spacing** - If growing in rows, plants should be 8 to 12 inches apart in rows at least 24 inches apart. If growing in beds, plants should be 8 - 12 inches apart in any direction.
- **Growing Temp** - Kale will germinate at 40 degrees but does best between 45 to 80 degrees. An excellent weather crop, it does better when temperatures are in the mid-60s to low 70s. It will grow in the 80s, but the growth slows, and when it reaches the 90s or above, it will bolt.
- **Pests** – Aphids and flea beetles are the two biggest concerns, along with any caterpillar.
- **Disease** - Kale suffers mainly from fungi-related diseases such as downy mildew, powdery mildew, and root rot.

The best defense is to water the soil and not the leaves and ensure that the ground has proper drainage.

- **Hardiness Zones** – Kale grows anywhere in North America. It can survive the summers in some northern states.
- **Tips** - Start kale a few weeks before the last heavy frost. A light frost tends to harden kale. To prolong the growing season, use a heavy mulch to protect the roots from freezing. Kale responds well to drip irrigation and does well in hydroponic settings.
- **Harvest** – Harvesting kale is optimal when the leaves are "hand-sized" – about 6 to 8 inches. Some people harvest smaller leaves and market them as baby kale. Kale regrows leaves throughout the growing season, making it a profitable item to sell. Harvest kale from the bottom up. It will encourage fresh leaves to grow and for the plant to increase in height. *Harvesting kale after the first frost allows the starches to turn to sugar, making kale more flavorful.*

Companion Plants

Kale plays well and benefits from the pest protection of garlic, onions, dill, nasturtium, and other mint family members. Basil, radishes, and mustard will help repel flea beetles. Nitrogen-loving plants such as clover, soybeans, snow peas, and other legumes will add nitrogen to the soil.

Kale does not play well with tomatoes and strawberries; a combination is more dangerous to tomatoes than to kale. Strawberries grow by producing runners. These runners will choke out competing plants, including kale.

Uses

Kale is a versatile food that can be the main attraction, a side dish, an appetizer, or juiced. Kale is very high in fiber and water, making it very healthy; it can help with many ailments from constipation to cancer.

When used in salads, kale adds texture, color, taste, and nutrients. Kale soup makes for a delicious low-calorie meal. When baked with olive oil and sea salt, kale makes for a crispy and tasty alternative to potato chips or chemically engineered items. This superfood becomes a super drink when juiced.

Good health depends on eating more whole foods and plants. Food choices affect everything from personal health to environmental health. The fate of the planet depends upon people eating more kale.

Fun Facts

- Kale has more vitamins than an orange.
- Kale has more calcium than milk.
- Kale has omega-3 fats.
- Kale has flavonoids that reduce the risk of stroke.

- Kale is available in green, white, purple, and bluish-green colors.
- Kale is a good source of lutein, which is good for eye health.
- Kale is a good source of iron, which helps spread oxygen throughout the body.
- Kale is the same thing as "Peasant's Cabbage."

Selected Varieties

Abyssinian Mustard is an heirloom often marketed as Ethiopian kale, or liki liki is an African variety. It is an oilseed variety. The leaves are like collard greens with a rich, buttery taste. The edible flower makes meals attractive, and butterflies are attracted to this flower, making it a great addition to any butterfly garden.

Blue Curled Scotch is a blue-green heirloom that only reaches 15 inches tall. While it is short, it is very hardy and can survive frost and even a light snowfall without losing its color. This productive variety is an excellent choice for growers that want food beyond the first frost. This kale dates to the late 1800s.

Dwarf Siberian Kale is a very cold hardy heirloom that does well after a frost and a few light snowfalls. This variety routinely survives winters in the south and produces for up to two years. It is not as tall or as wide as other varieties growing only 16 inches tall and maybe 18 inches wide. It is an ancient variety from Russia.

Cabbage Nero di Toscana is an heirloom from the Tuscany region of Italy. Dating back to the early 1800s, farmers marketed this kale as a tall, headless cabbage. This plant grows 24 inches wide and produces savory leaves great for quiche, soups, and salads.

Halbhoher Gruner Krauser is a German heirloom. This cold-hardy plant will make it through most southern winters. This kale can be cooked or eaten raw with great flavor. It grows to 18 inches tall. It is short but has longevity.

Madeley kale is a cold-hardy heirloom from England. Gardeners report that this variety is one of the most productive of the heirloom varieties. In addition to being a great grower, this kale is very flavorful. This variety came to the Americas through the Seed Ambassadors of Great Britain, a group dedicated to saving heirloom and open-pollinated seeds.

Ornamental Fringed Mix kale is a flowering heirloom that is attractive. This kale has white, pink, and purple leaves. People use this kale as a garnish in addition to cooking it as greens. Cool-weather brings out the color in this plant.

Russian Red Kale, also known as Ragged Jack Kale, is an heirloom dating back to the mid-1880s. It is a cold hardy plant that produces a mild and tender red-tinted leaf, and it is a superb choice for soups or quiches. It is easy to grow.

Scarlet Kale is an heirloom that is more purple than red; the color comes from its abundance of anthocyanin. This flavorful kale does better in warmer climates. It is light frost tolerant, but heavy frost or snow will kill it. It is a splendid variety that provides magnificent color to any kale collection.

Sea Kale (Crambe Maritima) is a tenacious heirloom from the hardened coast of Western Europe. This variety grows from the North Atlantic down to the Black Sea. This salt-tolerant kale still grows wild. Sailors used to pickle the greens for long sea voyages as a scurvy preventative, hence the nickname scurvy grass. This kale is the most drought-hardy variety of kale, and even bad gardeners can succeed with it.

Tronchuda Kale is a Portuguese heirloom. It is one of the more heat-hardy kales. The leaves of this variety are round, large, and flat. This kale tastes more like cabbage and is a cabbage substitute.

Eggplants

"How can people say they don't eat eggplant when God loves the color and the French love the name? I don't understand."
~ Jeff Smith

Eggplant is a renaissance vegetable representing usefulness, versatility, and greatness. Like the renaissance men of the past who were well-rounded and productive, so is this fruit.

Specialized knowledge is good, but technical expertise in many areas is better. Eggplants remind us of a time when people were inspired to do more and to be more – a period needing resurrection. The history of eggplants and their connection to this time should move people towards greatness. People should not go through life limited to just one pursuit.

New experiences bring joy to life. Life is more engaging when generating knowledge. When life is full of discoveries, it is as divine as eggplant.

Eggplant is a Solanaceae or nightshade family member, which includes tomatoes, potatoes, and peppers. Eggplants do well in warm weather and are not frost tolerant. They come in many different colors, such as purplish-black, white, orange, or green.

When harvesting eggplants, seek fruits with glossy, thin skin. Eggplant harvest may begin when fruits are small, but fruits should reach full size before harvesting. The best eggplants have firm cream-colored flesh with immature seeds.

History

Eggplant is originally from India, where it grows wild. In the wild, eggplants are spiny, bitter, orange, and pea-sized fruit — the modern and delicious eggplant results from thousands of years of careful and deliberate cultivation and selective breeding.

Eggplants have been an essential ingredient in Indian and Chinese food for over 1,500 years. Eggplants reached Japan during the Tang dynasty. They quickly spread throughout Japan and became a vital part of the diet.

The Japanese believed that eggplants were magical and had beneficial medical properties. In Japan, eggplant established itself as a solution for digestive issues, dental problems, and other injuries.

The English word for eggplant dates to India's British occupation because they thought it resembled an egg. Thus the name eggplant. Trade routes developed, introducing the eggplant to Europe. The French carried the eggplant to North Africa. The Spanish conquistadors brought the seeds to the New World, where they grew in popularity. Today, eggplants are very popular throughout North America.

Competitive Advantage

According to the USDA, eggplant represents a 100 million dollar a year business opportunity. It performs well in markets with Asian influences. Eggplants come in various shapes and colors and find their way into many different dishes.

Eggplant is a great meat replacement making it an outstanding featured dish, but it also does well in a supporting role. The internet is full of easy to use eggplant recipes, providing a rich source of eggplant marketing material.

For growers with a commercial kitchen or farm store, eggplant can become a high dollar premade item for customers. For example, eggplant parmesan provides growers a profitable, time-saving product for customers.

Marketing and Sales Strategies

Focus marketing on taste, usability, and health benefits. There are many different types of eggplants, each with a slightly different flavor and appearance. Farm-raised eggplants grown in natural soil taste better than hydroponically grown eggplants from a greenhouse.

Display eggplant prominently. Do not stack eggplants more than two high to avoid bruising. Various sizes, shapes, and colors of eggplant create a dynamic display. For maximum impact, place eggplant next to squash for color contrast. Purple eggplants contrast nicely with red produce such as tomatoes or peppers.

Sales strategies need to highlight the use of eggplant as a meat substitute. It would also be beneficial to have many different recipes and cooking tips. Grilling season is a great time to introduce eggplant as a grilling item. Lastly, think of value-added options such as prepared dishes with eggplants that customers can just heat and serve.

Production and growing

- **Soil and pH** - Eggplants need warm, moist soil that is loose with lots of organic material. The optimal pH for eggplant is pH 5.5 to 6.5.
- **Nutrients** - Eggplants are heavy feeders that need a constant supply of nutrients. For best results, eggplants need nitrogen (N), potassium (K), phosphorus (P), and magnesium (Mg).
- **Water** - eggplants need moist soil but not wet soil. Eggplants require 1-inch of water per week, with more during hot and dry conditions.
- **Spacing** - If growing in rows, eggplants should be 18 to 24 inches apart in rows 24 - 36 inches apart. If growing in beds, eggplants should be 18 to 24 inches apart in all directions.

- **Growing Temp** - Eggplants require warm weather and are not frost tolerant. Eggplants do best with daytime temperatures in the 80s to 90s and nighttime temperatures in the 70s.
- **Pests** - The most common eggplant pests are the tomato hornworm, eggplant mites, aphids, and cutworms.
- **Disease** - Cercospora leaf spot is a fungal disease that affects the leaves and stems of eggplants. Symptoms include small, circular yellow lesions on the foliage. Anthracnose Fruit Rot, sometimes called ripe fruit rot, is a fungal disease that often remains symptomless until it is ripe and ready to harvest.
- **Hardiness Zones** - Eggplant grows well in zones 5 - 12 and will grow as a perennial in zones 10-11.
- **Tips** - Use mulch with finely ground leaves or bark to help keep the soil moist and cool. Keep the ground free from weeds — stake eggplants to keep them from falling over when at maximum production.
- **Harvest -** Eggplants require daily picking. It encourages new fruit production. When removing the fruit, leave at least 1 inch of the calyx to help prevent rot. Eggplants are best when the skin is glossy and when your thumb does not leave an imprint.

Companion Plants

Eggplants need nitrogen and can benefit from legumes. Planting with peas and beans provides eggplants with sufficient nitrogen. Bush beans are usually a great choice because bush beans repel certain beetles while providing nitrogen. Many herbs are also useful as pest repellents when planted with eggplants.

Eggplants are members of the nightshade family, and they need to avoid tomatoes, peppers, and other nightshade plants because they share the exact soil requirements. They also attract many of the same pests and are susceptible to many of the same diseases.

Uses

Eggplant is popular because of its taste and health benefits. Cuisines such as eggplant parmesan, grilled eggplant, and eggplant sandwiches are on menus across the country. Eggplant has found its way into meatballs, meatloaves, kebabs, steaks, and burgers. Using eggplant as a meat substitute is an excellent way for people to increase their fiber intake while reducing calories.

Eggplant has many medical benefits. It aids with weight loss management because it is low in calories. A cup of eggplant has only 20 calories and a low amount of fat. Eggplant boasts a long list of nutritional benefits; it is a good source of dietary fiber, vitamin B1, copper, manganese, vitamin B6, niacin, potassium, folate, and vitamin K.

Fun Facts

- As part of her "bride price," a woman must have at least 12 eggplant recipes before her wedding day in China.
- In Turkey, "imam bayeldi" is a tasty treat of stuffed eggplant simmered in olive oil.
- When first introduced in Italy, people believed that anyone who ate the "mad apple" was sure to go insane.
- Eggplant seeds contain nicotine.
- Eggplant has a spiny stem that can grow from 16 to 57 inches in height.
- Eggplants are self-pollinating.
- Eggplants are berries.
- Juice made of leaves and roots of eggplant treats throat and stomach disorders, coughs, asthma, toothaches, and rheumatism.
- Delphinidin is a substance isolated from eggplant that exhibits anti-tumor properties.
- China is the largest grower of eggplants in the world.

Selected Varieties

Antigua Eggplant is an attractive white heirloom eggplant. This plant's violet/purple streaks fade to soft lavender to create a lovely fruit. This eggplant will grow to around 8 inches long and 3 inches wide. The flesh is white, tender, and mild tasting. This vigorous plant produces fresh fruit until the first frost. The English brought this eggplant to the Caribbean, where it made its way to the North American mainland.

Arumugam's Eggplant is an Indian heirloom. This plant produces green, white, and lavender-colored striped fruit. The name "Arumugam" comes from the Arumugam family of Ambal, India. The family would feed friends and travelers this eggplant and shared seeds with visitors. This Eggplant is a rare delicacy that is delicious in stews, curries or stuffed.

Astrakom Eggplant is a Russian heirloom designed for short seasons or cooler climates. This eggplant produces a deep purple fruit that looks like a stretched teardrop. These fruits are smaller than other eggplants and available for harvesting earlier.

These compact plants produce an abundance of small to medium-size fruit that is around 4 inches long. The astrakom is perfect for people who like petite fruit or do not have room for large fruits. Marketing this eggplant for individual use is effective. The size makes this an appealing main course when sliced, stuff, or plated. This variety is excellent for urban farmers using containers or bed growing.

Aswad Eggplant is a sizeable Iraqi heirloom. The fruit can weigh up to 3 pounds without becoming bitter. This eggplant is a great meat substitute that does exceptionally well on the grill. It tender and tasty.

Black Beauty Eggplant is a trendy heirloom plant. Introduced in the early 1900s, this plant quickly became popular due to its speed to harvest, which is only 95 days. The Black Beauty produces classic, large, oval, purple-black eggplants on broad plants. This fruit's durable shelf life makes it great for transporting and selling.

Cambodian Green Giant Eggplant is a large, round heirloom with slightly ribbed skin, giving the fruit more texture and appeal. Cambodian fruit is a full-flavored eggplant that is quick to mature (typically 75 - 80 days). It is somewhat cool tolerant; making it better for the north through any frost will kill it.

Casper Eggplant is a white, ghostlike heirloom that is friendly to the taste buds. This compact plant produces fruit up to 6 inches long. Casper is rarely bitter and has a very mild flavor. It is a thin-skinned fruit and does not require peeling when small. This white fruit juxtaposes nicely with dark purple or black varieties.

Cannibal Tomato Eggplant is an attractive plant with a shocking history. This plant produces a bitter-tasting tomato-appearing fruit that cannibals made into a sauce to use with human meals. The edible leaves of this eggplant are cooked like greens. This eggplant is native to Fiji and Tahiti, which accounts for its bitter taste.

Cookstown Orange Eggplant is typically an ornamental heirloom. The fruit is often bitter, even at a young age. This bitterness offers a culinary challenge and may be suited for chefs wishing to show off their culinary prowess. The Cookstown orange produces a squashed-looking round fruit with green stripes.

Fairytale Eggplant is a tiny purple heirloom that is as attractive as it is delicious. There is no need to peel this thin-skinned fruit when grilling, baking, or roasting. The fairytale eggplant is easy to grow, cook, and store. There are many opportunities with this fruit, and it has an inspired name for marketing.

Ichiban Eggplant is a long, slender dark purple heirloom from Asia. It is a dietary fiber source packed with vitamins and minerals, including vitamin C, folate, potassium, and manganese. Each of these works together to give this eggplant an almost black appearance. This eggplant has remarkable taste, is mild tasting, and perfect for Asian-infused dishes and splitting, grilling, or roasting.

Listada de Gandia Eggplant is an Old Italian heirloom from the Mediterranean region that is the darling of culinary and heirloom purists. This fruit is purple and white and is perfect for those who like Mediterranean cuisine. This fruit has a classic teardrop shape and produces small to medium-sized fruits.

Little Fingers Eggplant is a slender heirloom that is a perfect griller. This tall plant produces finger-sized fruits. The whole fingers are easy to cook, making them ideal for stir-fry style dishes. This product is a good pickler for a profitable value-added product. These fruits are seldom bitter and grow exceptionally well.

Long Purple Eggplant is the classic heirloom. It first appeared in seed catalogs in 1855, and it has been a favorite for over a century. This deep purple fruit has a bulging round end. This plant is a hardy grower that is quick to mature; a very productive plant. When harvested young, the skin is thin and pleasant with just a few seeds in the flesh.

Morden Midget Eggplant is a cold-tolerant heirloom released in 1958. This small plant yields a purple striped fruit that looks like little balls. This plant is well matched for cooler climates because its shorter size allows the plant to focus its energy on producing fruits quicker than other varieties. For its size, it is a heavy producer and does well in beds or containers.

Rosita Eggplant is an heirloom from Puerto Rico in the 1940s. This eggplant has pink/lavender fruit that is 8 inches long and 3 inches wide. The Rosita is sweeter than most other eggplants, and the skin is tender and hardly bitter.

Rosa Bianca Eggplant is a popular heirloom in culinary circles. This Italian variety produces a fruit with a mild-tasting flesh, and it is a popular centerpiece for many dishes. The mild taste allows for deeper seasoning absorption, particularly when grilling or roasting. The fruits have a rosy lavender color with a ring of white around the stem. This variety makes any farm stand more attractive.

Thai Round Green Eggplant is a viral heirloom from Thailand, known as the "Petch Parisa." This plant produces lime fruit with cream stripes. Common in Asian cuisine. The Thai round green is popping up in many Asian food stores and specialty markets on the west coast, gaining popularity across the nation.

Thai Yellow Eggplant is a popular Thailand variety that turns yellow or gold when it ripens. It makes for an attractive fruit that is the centerpiece for many Asian-inspired dishes. This eggplant is an excellent addition to any display as it is very eye-catching.

Turkish Orange Eggplant is a bright red heirloom that is a 3-inch ball. It is trendy in its home country of Turkey and the Mediterranean region. This old eggplant is from the 15th century. This sweet-tasting fruit can be roasted or baked. These small plants are heavy producers that crave the heat.

Zebra Eggplant is a purple heirloom with white stripes. It is an eggplant that has a visually alluring fruit that is 7-inches long and 3-inches wide. The Zebra eggplant is delicate and mild with white flesh. It is an excellent choice because of its appearance and production capacity.

Lettuce

"Lettuce is like a conversation: It must be fresh and crisp and so sparkling that you scarcely notice the bitter in it." ~ **C.D. Warner**

Crisp lettuce is confident. Crisp lettuce is effective. It is efficient and agile. *It is excellence in action,* and excellence must be an heirloom grower's goal. The produce marketplace is competitive, and the best option for any competitive endeavor is excellence.

Crisp lettuce is a reminder to perform at the highest level. Crisp lettuce is a reminder to stay cool under pressure. Crisp lettuce is a reminder that working well with others requires supporting others in the same way lettuce supports salad ingredients.

Individual salad ingredients have unique strengths and qualities, just as every person has unique strengths and qualities. When working together to form salad, lettuce is not trying to overpower its teammates; instead, its goal is to support its teammates.

Lettuce is an annual that grows well in cool weather and may even tolerate a light frost. Lettuce quickly grows and is ready to harvest in only 30 days. Lettuce does well in the ground; however, many people grow it using hydroponic techniques. One advantage to using hydroponics is it helps keeps the roots cool, allowing them to sustain warmer temperatures.

Lettuce harvest occurs when the head has reached full size just before maturity. Young and tender lettuce has the best taste. Maturing lettuce becomes bitter and unpleasant. To maximize yield, try removing outer leaves so that the center leaves can continue to grow.

Harvest butterhead or romaine lettuces by removing the outer leaves, digging up the whole plant, or cutting the plant about an inch above the soil surface. Harvest crisphead lettuce when the center is firm.

History

The first recorded users of lettuce were the Egyptians. The Egyptians used lettuce seeds for oil production for religious rituals. At the Egyptians' time, lettuce grew 3 feet tall and was stalky like bolted lettuce.

Around 600 BC, lettuce seed made its way to Greece. Greeks began selectively breeding lettuce into the edible plant we recognize today. After the Romans conquered Greece, lettuce made its way to Rome and then spread to Europe.

Lettuce, during Middle Ages, was thought to more pharmaceutical purposes than nutritional value. It was because of Hildegard of Bingen, the founder of scientific natural history in Germany, who wrote extensively about lettuce and its medicinal properties.

The acceptance of lettuce as mainstream food came during the Renaissance period. Joachim Camerarius, the father of modern lettuce, championed lettuce and developed the descriptions of the three basic modern lettuces: head lettuce, loose-leaf lettuce, and romaine lettuce.

Christopher Columbus brought lettuce to the Americas from Europe in the late 15th century. The Age of Enlightenment brought many new scientific discoveries – discoveries that included new lettuce varieties.

In the mid-1900s, salads increased in popularity to lose weight. Over the following decades, salads became more than a weight-loss item. Salads have become the main course and often featured food as part of a healthy diet.

Competitive Advantage

Lettuce is inexpensive and quick to grow (30 days). The loose-leaf varieties provide continuous harvesting, and both types provide early cash flow. Lettuce is also a great late season product that allows growers to extend their growing season.

A competitive advantage that many people overlook with lettuce is premade salads. Virtually all grocery stores have premade salads in the deli section, as well as all restaurants. Salads are big businesses, and by offering premade salads, growers can create a value-added product without much effort. If a grower wanted to be competitive, they could provide salad delivery to businesses.

Marketing and Sales Strategies

The key to marketing and selling lettuce is keeping the product fresh. Lettuce wilts when exposed to the sun and wind.

Packaging is critical. The packaging of lettuce needs to serve dual purposes. First, it needs to keep the product fresh. Secondly, it needs to attract the attention of the customer.

Knowing lettuce history and key lettuce facts is essential for successful marketing. The more you know about the type of lettuce you are growing, the better you will sell it. People buy compelling stories. Talk about the origins of lettuce, its history, health benefits, and have different varieties that have contrasting colors.

Production and growing

- **Soil and pH** - lettuce does best in loose sandy loam soil. Lettuce also does well without soil and maybe grown hydroponically. The optimal pH for lettuce is 6.0 to 6.5.
- **Nutrients** - Lettuce is easy to grow. It just needs nitrogen. For continuous harvesting, lettuce needs phosphorus (P) and potassium (k) for leaf regrowth.
- **Water** - Lettuce is 90 percent water – so it needs a steady supply of water. The soil should remain moist but not wet. On average, lettuce needs the equivalent of one inch per week.

- **Spacing** - If planting in rows and the leaves will be harvested, it should be planted 12 to 16 inches apart in rows 18 inches apart. If harvesting the entire plant space, it 4 to 6-inches apart. If growing hydroponically or in rows, lettuce should be 4-6 inches apart in all directions.
- **Growing Temp** - lettuce is a cool weather plant. Lettuce seeds will germinate around 34 degrees. The optimal growing temperature is 45 to 80. It grows slow when the temperature is below 45, and when temperatures are above 80, it will bolt.
- **Pests** - Aphids are problematic, as well as all categories of caterpillars. Leaf miners are problematic.
- **Disease** - Downy Mildew is a problem; the primary symptoms are yellowish or light green areas on the leaves' upper surface. Tip burn and soft rot are other hazards for lettuce.
- **Hardiness Zones** - Since lettuce is a fast grower, it can be grown in almost all zones if planted 60 days before temperatures get into the 80s or above.
- **Tips** - For a continuous harvest, plant lettuce every two weeks until the season is over. When getting ready for fall planting, plant lettuce and cover with straw or hay during August to maintain moisture. To extend the growing season, plant late lettuce in the shade.
- **Harvest** – Pick lettuce when it just reaches full size but just before maturity. Lettuce is best when it is young and tender. Harvest butterhead or romaine lettuces by removing outer leaves, digging up the whole plant, or cutting the plant about an inch above the soil surface.

Harvest crisphead when the center is firm. Lettuce gets bitter and woody as it ages and it will go rancid quickly, so check your garden daily.

Companion Plants

Lettuce plays well with carrots, cucumber, onions, beets, and marigolds. Onion and beets have shallow roots, and planting lettuce helps crowd out weeds before they grow. Trellised cucumbers provide shade for the lettuce helping to extend the growing season. Marigolds aid in pest control.

Lettuce does not play well with strawberries. Strawberries will choke out lettuce. Lettuce and potatoes struggle when planted side by side.

Uses

Lettuce's most popular use is as a salad. The best salads are lettuce mixed with various greens such as kale, vegetables, meats, and cheeses. Romaine lettuce is the go-to lettuce for Caesar salads, but lettuce is not limited to salads. It is the perfect addition to sandwiches. Leaf lettuce makes a healthy wrap, and adding lettuce to soups is always a tasty and healthy option.

Lettuce has nonfood uses in medicine. For example, lettuce has anti-inflammatory properties. It is a cholesterol reducer, reducing the risk for heart attack and stroke. People have long used lettuce as a sleep aid. The fiber in lettuces reduces or eliminates constipation. For over a century, lettuce has been the food of choice to reduce and manage weight. Lastly, lettuce is useful in the fight against cancer.

Fun Facts

- Lettuce comes from the Latin word "lactuca."
- Lettuce is a member of the daisy family.
- Lettuce is a good source of Omega 3.
- Lettuce is the second most popular fresh vegetable in the US behind potatoes.
- Lettuce is also known as *rabbit food,* a term coined in the 1930s.
- Lettuce has a glycemic index of 15.
- One cup of lettuce has nine calories and 1.3 grams of fiber.
- Lettuce contains small amounts of lactucarium, a mild sedative.
- Americans eat, on average, 33 pounds of lettuce each year.
- Face washing with lettuce extract is good for skin health and care.
- China is the world's largest producer of lettuce.
- California produces more than 75% of the nation's head lettuce.

- Iceberg lettuce makes up 73% of all the lettuce grown in the United States.
- Caesar salad originated in Mexico.
- The world's largest salad weighed 41,998 pounds.
- Thomas Jefferson had 19 varieties of lettuce growing in his garden at Monticello.
- Crushed ice gave Iceberg lettuce its name during the 1920s.
- Oilseed lettuce produces large oil-packed seeds and is the oldest lettuce.
- Stem lettuce is grown for its stalks and used primarily in Asian cooking.

Selected Varieties

Amerikanischer Brauner Lettuce is a Pennsylvania Dutch heirloom variety from the 1870s. This lettuce has crimped and deeply ruffled dark green leaves tinged with bronze. It grows well in cool weather and produces nine-inch diameter heads. The dark and striking colors of this lettuce make it an excellent choice for marketing.

Amish Deer Tongue Lettuce is a green heirloom with triangular leaves. This lettuce is excellent for baby salad greens and pairs well with other varieties such as arugula. These leaves are loose, and it is slow bolting, allowing for a more extended season. It is an old favorite among the Amish community and has great potential in many markets.

Arugula or Arugula Rocket Lettuce is more of a mustard green heirloom than lettuce; it is included here because of its use and listing in most seed catalogs. This cabbage family member is often listed with lettuce because of its use — a trendy culinary item found in restaurants across the country. The arugula is peppery in flavor and is a superfood. Always a good seller and necessary when selling salad mixes.

Australian Yellow Lettuce is a bright yellow-green loose-leaf heirloom from the land down under. This lettuce is heat tolerant and slow to bolt, making this a great option to extend the growing period. This lettuce starts yellow and turns green as it matures. The Australian yellow lettuce has a spinach taste making it an excellent add-in for most salad mixes.

Ballon Lettuce is a romaine heirloom from the 1800s. The Ballon lettuce has light green frilly leaves in heads about 10 inches tall and 8 inches wide. It is one of the larger and rarer lettuce heirlooms available.

Big Boston Lettuce is a French heirloom that came to America in the late 1800s. Big Boston's name was a marketing idea to promote it because it is a large, tender butterhead lettuce.

Bronze beauty Lettuce is an all-American heirloom. This lettuce produces sweet leaves painted with a maroon color around the edge of the wavy leaf margins. The name is from an award given to the Germain's Seed Co at the 1947 All-America Selections. This lettuce is slow to bolt, grows well in the south, and produces deep into the north's summer.

Celtuce Lettuce is an ancient Chinese heirloom. This lettuce is strong-flavored with leaves that are long and tapered. This lettuce has long celery-like stalks. These edible stalks are crunchy and do well in soups. The leavers are dual-purpose and may be used raw in a salad or treated as traditional greens. This lettuce has more vitamin C than most other varieties. It is an attention-getter and a great conversation starter for marketplaces.

Crisphead Lettuce or iceberg is the most grown lettuce in America. This lettuce has tightly packed heads that resemble a cabbage and has a very high water content little flavor. This lettuce is easy to grow and ships well under ice. It is excellent for a grower that ships long distances. Growers looking for something unique to sell locally may want to consider something different.

Crisp mint Lettuce is a romaine heirloom whose name comes from its looks, not its taste. It has large mint-green outer leaves that enclose its crystal-white hearts with a bland taste but crunchy texture. The heads grow to 10 inches in height; this lettuce displays well in the garden and the produce stand.

Devil's Ear Lettuce is a French heirloom also called "Les Oreilles du Diable." The Devil's ear lettuce has large, spreading, loose-leaf lettuce with hints of burgundy. It has a nutty and bitter-free taste with a crisp texture. This good grower is slow to bolt and sustains well in the garden.

Forellenschluss Lettuce is an Austrian heirloom. It also goes by the name "bunte forellenschluss." Bunte is German for colorful, and forellenschluss is Austrian for speckled trout. Butterhead lettuce has apple green leaves with maroon speckles. It could be marketed under the name speckled trout or speckled lettuce. For more of a branding effect, this could call this *your farm name's* speckled trout lettuce. Talk about a conversation starter!

Garnet Rose Lettuce is a bright garnet red heirloom with savoy leaves. This lettuce is the reddest of the Romaine lettuces because of its increased concentration of anthocyanin. The Garnet Rose is slow to bolt with excellent uniformity. It adds color to salads, farm stands and even does well in flowerbeds.

Gentilina Lettuce is a bright green Italian heirloom with fizzled, leafy heads. It has above-average resistance to bolting. The leaves of this plant are tender, flavorful, and crisp making it a great salad choice. The Latin root of this lettuce translates into "nobility of spirit," which is a suitable description of this lettuce.

Grandpa Admire's Lettuce is a heat-tolerant butterhead heirloom. This lettuce forms large plants with large, loose heads with crinkled bronze-tinted/splashed leaves. This delicious lettuce displays wells.

Henderson's Black Seeded Lettuce is a light yellow-green heirloom from the 1870s by Peter Henderson & Co. Sometimes called the black seeded Simpson. This lettuce is well suited for a wide range of climates and grows in all North American zones. This plant is slow to bolt and is one of the more heat-tolerant lettuces available.

Ice Queen Lettuce is a crisphead/iceberg French heirloom called "Reine des Glace" in French. It has incredible tolerance to cold weather does great when planted extra early or late. The ruffled outer leaves are mild enough to use for leaf-lettuce or harvest as baby greens. This lettuce is much better tasting than the plain iceberg variety because of its darker green color. The only drawback is the interior tends to be bitter, however many people consider it the best crisphead lettuce.

Landis Winter Lettuce is a dark green heirloom from the Pennsylvania Dutch. A direct descendant of the white tennis ball lettuce that was popular in the 1700s. The Landis winter is one of the more frost-resistant lettuces varieties. It can survive light snow or heavy frost. It is a big one that can grow 12-inches in diameter!

Lamb Lettuce is a slow-growing heirloom that holds up well in cold weather. This easy-to-grow lettuce does fine in poor soil. The lamb lettuce produces green leaves that look like a lamb's tongue. The leaves have a tangy flavor. Also known as Corn Salad because the long spoon-shaped leaves look like cornhusks. An excellent choice for salads or when cooked like greens.

Lollo Bionda Lettuce is a classic European heirloom. This lettuce produces attractive lime-green leaves that are tight, curly, and compact. Many seed companies marketed this as "coral lettuce." There is a red version known as Lollo Bionda Rosa; these lettuces offer a visually appealing salad full of color, texture, and volume when used in combination.

Lunix Lettuce is an oak leaf heirloom. This lettuce produces deep red leaves and is very slow to bolt. This lettuce does great when grown hydroponically or when grown in a greenhouse or hoop house. This rare variety is attractive and delicious.

Mascara Lettuce is a frilly red oak leaf heirloom that holds its color well and is slow to bolt. This lettuce is stunning with its mascara-red leaves. It is one of the brightest and most beautiful oak-shaped types on the market. Developed in Holland, this lettuce has great marketing potential in America.

May Queen Lettuce is a delicate butterhead style and a classic European heirloom. Its tender yellow hearts and light green leaves provide a sweet and traditional flavor. The May Queen is a quick grower with medium-sized heads. This lettuce was popular in Europe during the 1800s. It is an excellent choice to market to chefs and farm-to-table restaurants.

Merlot Lettuce is one of the darkest red of all lettuces. The reason is it has the highest level of anthocyanin (antioxidant) of any lettuce variety. This leaf lettuce has wavy and frilly leaves that are both crisp and waxy. It has good bolt resistance and cold tolerance. This heirloom is well suited to be a late fall to winter crop. Many growers treat this as a cut and grow again plant.

Merveille Des Quatre Saisons Lettuce is an old French heirloom with a great marketing name. This French name promises a refined and eloquent gourmet product, and its crisp and tender reddish leaves fulfill that promise. This lettuce is great to market to food lovers and chefs.

Mignonette Bronze Lettuce is an excellent choice for hot and tropical weather. This heirloom is very slow to bolt. This lettuce has frilled leaves with bronze-green heads that are 8 inches wide. The Mignonette Bronze dates to the 1880s and has been a popular market variety for over a century. Many growers do well with this lettuce at market because of its looks and taste.

Oakleaf Lettuce is a French variety from the 1770s. The French company Vilmorin is the first recorded marketer of this variety. This lettuce looks like a cluster of oak leaves on a stalk. Many of today's current oak varieties descended from this heirloom—this an exceptional add-in for a spring salad. The leaves are green and burgundy or bronze.

Oilseed Lettuce is the oldest continuously grown heirloom. This Egyptian lettuce, whose seeds are 35% oil, is used for oil production. Its oil has many uses, including cooking, skincare, and soap making. Lettuce seed oil can sell for up to $20.00 an ounce, making this a profitable product. Oilseed's few leaves, while edible, are dull.

Pablo Lettuce is a Batavian heirloom with green leaves and bright bronze-purple tints in the center. From the delta, formed by the Rhine and Maas rivers. This plant produces lettuce that is mild, crisp and juicy, and very slow to bolt. This lettuce is baby lettuce when picked young or head lettuce when matured.

Parris Island Cos Lettuce is a Romaine heirloom introduced by Ferry-Morse in 1951. The leaves of this lettuce are both crisp and sweet. This lettuce is very popular in the South East but does well anywhere. This lettuce is uniform with upright leaves perfect for holding dips, dressing, or using as a wrap.

Red Velvet Lettuce is a soft frilled maroon and green loose-leaf heirloom. It is a good cut and grow vegetable – an excellent item for maximizing yields and profits. This lettuce adds nice color and texture to the marketing mix. The red velvet is a slow bolter and does much better in the spring than in the fall.

Rouge d'Hiver Lettuce is a French heirloom adding piquancy and sharpness to meals. It is a noteworthy complement to salad mixes, sandwiches, or a garnish whose first mention was in Vilmorin's vegetable garden book from 1885. It has red and green leaves that turn a darker shade of red as the weather cools.

Romaine Lettuce is a tall green head of lettuce filled with nutrients. This heirloom is one of the most popular lettuces in the USA and very marketable. This lettuce has a deep taste and is very versatile. It is very heat tolerant, slow to bolt, and easy to grow. Another name for Romaine lettuce is cos lettuce.

Rouge Grenobloise Lettuce is a red-tinted crisphead Batavian heirloom from France. This lettuce has an exquisite flavor, is cold tolerant, and slow to bolt – a fast-growing plant that is a great producer. This plant can grow during mild southern winters.

Sanguine Ameliore Lettuce is a 19th-century French heirloom brought to America by C. C. Morse in the early 1900s. Originally known as "Strawberry Cabbage Lettuce," this is a butterhead style lettuce. This alluring lettuce has smooth, medium-size emerald leaves splashed with scarlet red speckles — tender and mild lettuce that does well in areas with mild winters.

Speckled Lettuce is a very Old Dutch heirloom from the 1700s. This lettuce is still popular with the Pennsylvania Amish. This lettuce has green apple-colored leaves that are speckled and splashed with deep red. This lettuce arrived in the New World when Urias Martin emigrated from the Netherlands to Ontario, Canada, in 1799.

Spotted Aleppo Syrian Lettuce is a "semi-Cos" heirloom with 8-10 inch upwardly spreading leaves covered with red dots and speckles. Extremely rare lettuce was introduced to England from Syria during the 1680s. It made it to America in 1786 by Philadelphia seedsman Peter Crouwells. It was grown at Monticello by Thomas Jefferson –historically significant lettuce.

Syrian Green Lettuce is an old heirloom that has green leaves and is crisp and crunchy in texture. It is a romaine lettuce with upward spreading leaves that are 6 to 7 inches tall. The head of this lettuce is about 8 inches across and needs more space than other lettuce varieties -- typically 10 to 12 inches. This lettuce is slow to bolt in hot weather and does well in South and Southwest areas.

Summer Crisp Lettuce is a French heirloom. A slow to bolt lettuce that stays crisp even in the warmer months. This lettuce produces moderately dense heads that are crunchy. This heirloom is in between a crisphead and loose-leaf type. The summer crisp is dual-purpose lettuce used as either baby lettuce or head lettuce.

Tennis ball Lettuce is a tiny heirloom producing loose heads that are 6-8 inches in diameter. Jefferson grew this lettuce at Monticello. This black-seeded lettuce is very easy to grow. People have enjoyed growing and eating this lettuce for centuries. It makes a great addition to any grower's product mix.

Tom Thumb Lettuce is classic heirloom lettuce from the 1850s. This lettuce produces small cabbage-like green heads that are only 3-4 inches across—a great item to market in larger cities where people have limited refrigeration space. Tom Thumb is a very marketable name, and growers report that this lettuce sells itself in many markets.

Silesian Lettuce is an old French heirloom that dates to the 1700s. It is texture, and crinkled leaves creates a striking appearance. This lettuce has a pale green color and produces heads with 10 to 12-inch diameters similar to Iceberg, but with a much improve flavor. In Europe, this variety remains popular; it finds its way into many traditional European dishes and is ready to be introduced to American food connoisseurs.

Melon

"Men and melons are hard to know" ~ **Benjamin Franklin**

Melons are the promise of summer. To plant a melon is to plant hope. Once the seed is in the ground, we have something to us motivated. We have a reason to keep working. Melons are a blissful treat, and melons are a reminder that simple things bring the greatest joy.

Summers cannot exist without melons. In season, melons are sweet, refreshing, and nature's treat. In season, melons bring people together in hopeful anticipation. In season, melons bring out the best in summer.

It takes three months of growing to get that wonderful, in-season melon, and the south provides the proper growing conditions. They can do well in the north with planning, work, and effort. This section focuses on cantaloupes, honeydews, and other specialty melons. *Watermelons have a separate chapter.*

Melons make a great snack, treat, or summer dessert.
Melons are perfect for people who spend time outdoors and need a rehydrating snack. Besides, melons are a great source of vitamins and minerals that combat heat fatigue.

The taste of melons is what most people think of when they think of melons. It is a guilt-free, easy dessert, snack, or meal. The mildly sweet and juicy flavor of cantaloupe makes it a perfect fruit for any eater.

Competitive Advantage

Melons are great to sell at farmers markets and have great merchandising appeal. An adage says, "Stack it high and watch it fly." Melons are great for stacking and always make an attractive display.

Melons have a great price point for both consumers and growers. Melons provide value to customers because they are large. Melons provide value to growers because they increase the sales average by being an expensive single item.

The key to moving melons is to focus on varieties that have visual and taste appeal. Most melons in the retail market do not necessarily taste great. Retailers are more concerned about shipping and longer shelf life than taste. Local growers are unique because they can focus on varieties that have a better flavor with attractive looks.

History

Africa is the home of melons. Egypt was the first recorded user of melons. Egyptians left seeds in tombs for loved ones to use in the afterlife, and artists recorded melon seeds in wall paintings.

Melons have been around since recorded history. Melons made their way around the world through trade with the ancient Greeks. From there, melons made their way to Asia and Europe. Columbus brought melons to Haiti, thus introducing melons to the New World on his second voyage. Melons made it to North America via the slave trade.

Marketing and Sales Strategies

People actively seek out melons during the summer. Of grocery store shoppers, 41% report having bought a melon in the past year. That is a considerable number of potential customers.

Most growers offer one or two types of standard melons. The variety of melons available allows you to provide a slightly different version of a familiar product. *Heirloom melons come with stories, and people buy stories.*

When introducing heirloom melons, offer samples. People like familiarity, but people also like uniqueness. A melon is a relatively significant produce investment, and people do not want to be stuck with something they do not like.

Offer fresh-cut options for customers. Many people just do not need a whole melon, nor do they want to deal with the mess of cutting up a melon. Promote melons heavily during the summer holidays. Offer different options for serving this popular fruit like smoothies, fruit salads, and even melon-flavored sherbet.

Production and growing

- **Soil and pH** - Melons grow well in sandy loam soil with high organic matter such as composted manure. The optimum pH for melons is 6.0 to 6.5.
- **Nutrients** – Nitrogen (N) fuels high yields. By boosting leaf growth, nitrogen promotes sugar accumulation in

melons. Phosphorus (P) is required for flowering and fruit filling. Potassium (K) and calcium (Ca) are necessary during fruit setting and fruit filling.

- **Water** - Melons require 1 to 2 inches of water every 7 to 10 days. Too much water at once will cause melons to burst.
- **Spacing** - Hills of muskmelon and honeydew should be spaced 1½ to 2 feet apart with 5 to 6 feet between rows.
- **Growing Temp** - Melon seeds germinate between 70 and 90 degrees.
- **Pests** - Pests are most critical in the seedling or early growth stage. Cucumber beetles, squash bugs, mites, and aphids are the most common melon pests.
- **Disease** - Foliar and root diseases can be problematic for melons. The two best preventions are air circulation and well-drained ground.
- **Hardiness Zones** - Melons grow in zones 3 – 11.
- **Tips** - When seedlings have 1 or 2 true leaves, thin to 2 or 3 well-spaced plants per hill.
- **Harvest -** When harvesting melons, look for fruit that will easily disconnect from the vine. For cantaloupes, skin color and stem are critical indicators of their readiness. When ripe, cantaloupes have a musky smell. Melons typically ripen over a short period. As soon as one melon is ready, the others will not be far behind.

Companion Plants

Plant marigolds with melons. Marigolds will stimulate growth while deterring bean beetles, aphids, potato bugs, squash bugs, nematodes, and maggots - all of which will want to snack on melons.

Corn is another good companion plant. Once melons are established, the vines will choke out or smother weeds that want to compete with melons. Okra is another great companion plant for the same reason. Typically, most tall plants do well with melons.

Lettuce and radishes, while low growing, tend to do well melons. Lettuce and radishes harvest are simultaneous with melon starting. It allows for better use of space, which is vital for urban growers. These early crops look inviting and suppress weed growth, making the melon patch easier to work.

Melons and potatoes do not grow well together. Potatoes are ready for harvest just as the melons start to grow and bear fruit. Potato harvesting requires digging, and there is no safe way to dig potatoes out of a melon patch.

Potato plants are at their peak height when it is time to plant to melons. It creates a sunblock, and melons require full sun. Potatoes are attractive to many melon-loving pests. Having these two plants together increases the risk of blight that can destroy both crops.

Uses

Melons are as healthy as they are tasty. They have massive quantities of beta-carotene, folic acid, potassium, vitamin C, and fiber. These things have many health benefits, such as lower cholesterol, lower stress, and weight management. Also, melons are a great source of vitamin B, the foundation of energy production. A diet high in vitamin B allows people to process sugars and carbs, especially harmful processed carbs, efficiently.

Melons are great for skincare. Melons help people with dry and rough skin. Honeydew, cantaloupe, and watermelon can tone skin and provide anti-aging benefits due to vitamins A, B, and C.

The most common use of melons is as a food. Melons are great by themselves, as part of a salad, or as a garnish. Melons are excellent for juices and drink making. Melon cocktails are fun and delicious. These refreshing drinks may use fresh melon juice, chunks of melon, cantaloupe, or honeydew mixed with liquor.

Fun Facts

- Melons are a type of berry.
- Melon compounds help in the fight against age-related macular degeneration.
- One cup of diced melon contains only 53 calories.
- Just 200 grams of melon meets the daily requirement of vitamin C.

- Melons are great add-ins to salads, smoothies, salsas, and adult drinks.
- The name cantaloupe comes from the Italian village of Cantalupo.
- The ancient Egyptians regarded the honeydew as sacred, reserving it for the elite.
- In China, the honeydew goes by Wallace melon because Vice President Henry Wallace distributed melon seeds to local farmers as a goodwill gesture.
- Yubari King Melons are the most expensive melons globally and grow only in a small region of Japan.
- Roasted melon seeds make a great snack.
- China produces over 8 million tons of melons each year.
- Traditional Chinese medicine uses all melon parts.
- Australians refer to cantaloupe as rockmelon.
- Cantaloupes are the most popular melon in the United States.
- Honeydew is one of the few melons that continues to ripen after harvest.
- Spain is the largest producer of melons in Europe.
- Cantaloupes are the easiest melons to determine ripeness because they fall off the vine.

Selected Varieties

Alacati Melon is a Turkish heirloom. People in Turkey regard this as a national treasure. It is a classic green and speckled variety with white flesh. This melon stores and transports well and has a great taste. The name comes from a Turkish seaside town famous for its fruit, vineyards, and windmills.

Amish Melon is an heirloom from the Dutch Amish. This muskmelon has everything people like about melons; it has yellow skin and orange flesh when ripe. This very prolific plant produces several fruits that average 4 to 7 pounds each. It is profitable and easy-grow.

Ananas D'Amerique A Chair Verte Melon is a fragrant heirloom that is sweet and delicious. Thomas Jefferson grew this melon at Monticello. The popularity of this melon peaked in the mid-1800s. The fruit has dark green or yellow skin, depending on its genetics that is becoming rare. This old heirloom needs saving by heirloom growers.

Ashkahadbad Melon is a honeydew heirloom from Turkmenistan. This variety deserves a chance. This melon has a rich sweet flavor with smooth golden skin with green flesh; it is a heavy producer of 8-10 lb. fruits. This melon is particularly well suited for areas that have Asian-inspired food trends and markets.

Banana Melon is a smooth yellow skin heirloom with a long oval shape that resembles a banana. This fruit is sweet with a subtle and somewhat spicy taste with pink flesh. This fruit grows 16 to 24 inches long and weighs 5 to 8 pounds. The unique shape makes a great display and conversation starter at any market.

Batee Smara Melon is a green heirloom from Iraq that produces brownish-green oblong fruits with lime green flesh. This fruit is a traditional favorite in the open-air markets of the Middle East. Sweet and tart with a dash of citrus, this melon is always a treat. The name comes from Smara and translates as "old melon." This variety is in danger of becoming extinct, and it needs new growers to save it.

Bidwell Casaba Melon is an heirloom that dates to the mid-1800s when the USDA gave this seed stock to farmers. Made famous by General John Bidwell, this melon produces a huge fruit that weighs up to 16 pounds and looks like green footballs – a sweet melon that makes a fabulous dessert.

Boule d' Melon is an old French heirloom from the late 1880s. It is a smooth sweet smooth melon with a rugged exterior. This melon ships well, is easy to grow and makes a great display. Popular in France among chefs, there is no reason this melon could not enjoy the same acceptance here. This melon is waiting for a grower to make it commercially viable.

Canoe Creek Colossal is an American heirloom from the banks of Canoe Creek, Florida. One of the largest melons, it grows up to 20 pounds. The vines only set a few fruits, so it is not as productive as other varieties, but these oversized fruits are very attention-getting. It is an excellent addition to any melon mix. This melon is yellow and green speckled when ripe with orange flesh.

Casaba Golden Beauty Melon is a Turkish heirloom. This melon made its way to America via Burrell's in 1927, who described it as a sweet white flesh melon with a tough golden rind about the same color as a green pear. This melon has a long shelf life, storing well into the winter. Very popular in Turkey but rare in America.

Charentais Melon is a French heirloom melon that is super sweet and fragrant. In the French countryside, where this melon is grown, people keep it around for its pleasant aroma. This melon has light grey/green skin with a hint of orange flesh. It does well in European markets where it commands a high price. This small melon weighs 2 to 4 pounds and is a perfect choice for markets whose customers need a small but flavorful product.

Eden's Gem or Rocky Ford is an heirloom muskmelon that dates to the late 1800s. It is the quintessential old-time muskmelon. This melon has the classic heavily netted rind with a sweet-tasting flesh that stores well. This muskmelon comes from the Rocky Ford area of Colorado, making it an all-American classic.

Escondido Gold Melon is a larger Israeli heirloom with an oblong shape. This melon is famous for its taste; it was trendy in the west during the middle of the last century. Like many heirlooms, this melon's popularity decreased not because of taste but because industrial growers prefer lighter, easier-to-ship melons. This melon is poised to make a comeback and does excellent in every market.

Ginger's Pride Melon is one of the largest heirlooms weighing up to 22 pounds. This melon is big and sweet and makes a great treat. This melon is the perfect family melon or for someone expecting a crowd. This large melon has the classic cantaloupe look and smell; it is a heavy producer with exceptional yields. Originating from Kentucky, this is a southern icon.

Golden Sweet Melon is an underutilized Asian heirloom with bright golden skin and white flesh with lots of natural sugar. It is melon easy to grow and highly prolific. A trendy item in Taiwan, it has been slow to gain traction in the United States. This melon provides an opportunity for growers to offer a unique and tasty product at market that competitors will not provide. It does well in markets with an Asian influence.

Hearts of Gold Melon is an heirloom melon that dates back to the 1880s. It was a popular melon during the early 1900s; however, as modernization took place and large farms crowded out small farms, this melon became rare. Also called a "hoodoo" melon. Both names offer good marketing potential.

Hithadhoo Maldives Melon is a very interesting heirloom; when young, it used like a cucumber. When large and ripe, it is a delicious melon. This melon is very rare outside of the Indian Ocean region. The USDA brought these seeds to the United States in the 1980s. Growers were not sure what to make of them because of their dual-use. It is an opportunity for creative and innovative growers to offer something unique.

Ineya Melong Melon is a Soviet Union heirloom producing uniform 6 to 8-inch fruit with a smooth-skinned, stiff, golden rind. The flesh is pale cream-colored, crunchy yet juicy. This heirloom has a honeydew flavor with hints of mulberry or banana. This melon does well in fruit salads, as a snack, or for breakfast.

Jenny Lind Melon is a tiny green-fleshed heirloom from the 1840s. Name after an 1800s Swedish singer. This melon produces 1 to 2-pound turban-shaped fruits that are very sweet. Unlike most other cantaloupes, its skin and flesh are light green.

Kajari Melon is an early Indian heirloom with copper-red with green and cream stripes. It is unusual, beautiful, and delicious with flesh that is sweet, aromatic, and slightly musky tasting. It is fun to grow, eat, and sell.

Keli Kheli Melon is an Indian heirloom. This bitter melon is slightly acidic. It is used in salads and looks impressive in the garden and marketplace because it is bright red and has yellow, irregular stripes. For growers looking for an alternative or natural medicine products, the Keli Kheli provides a product for people searching for natural psoriasis treatment.

Mango Melon or vine peach is an heirloom melon that dates to the 1880s. The fruits have the size, shape, and color of an orange but with a mango's texture. This melon produces a watery fruit; it is a cooking melon suited for preserves, pie filling, or pickling. The fruits store extremely well after picking. The vines of this plant are vigorous and productive. When ripe, the fruits slip freely from the stems. It is an excellent item for experimentation.

Missouri Gold Melon is an old southern heirloom from Missouri. This super sweet melon does well in the south. This melon produces fruits that are 2 to 3 pounds each and will do so in abundance. These melons are perfect personal melons.

Noir de Carmes Melon is a black French heirloom from the 1700s. Carmelite monks are responsible for the development and saving of this melon. This black melon with orange flesh is a contrasting work of art. This melon has deep ribs with smooth skin. These fruits typically weigh 3 to 6 pounds each and are a standout in any farmer's market.

Petit Gris de Rennes Melon is a French heirloom introduced by a Bishop of Rennes 400 years ago. The name means "little grey," which describes the appearance just before ripening. The fruits of this small melon weigh 2-3 pounds and have a mustard and olive speckled rind. This unique tasting melon has an orange and brown sugar taste.

Plum Granny Melon is an heirloom that goes by many different names, such as Queen Anne Pocket Melon, Vine Pomegranate, and Perfume Melon. During the Victorian-era, this melon masked body odor as people carried it in pockets or purses. This small, apple-sized melon is yellow with orange stripes and white flesh. This melon tastes more like a raw cucumber and is not very sweet.

Valencia Winter Melon is an heirloom that has staying power. If kept cool, it can store for up to four months. It arrived in America during the 1830s from Spain. This melon does well in cooler climates, tastes excellent, and ships well. It is a good option for northern growers and growers who want something unique.

Okra

"I always like summer best. You can eat fresh corn from daddy's garden, and okra, and greens, and cabbage." ~ **Nikki Giovanni**

When the summer gets hot, okra gets going. Okra is an excellent example of how to thrive in adverse conditions. When okra is at its peak, many other garden items are struggling. Okra hits adversity head-on and does not waiver. Adversity brings out the best in okra.

People should be more like okra. Adversity is nothing more than an opportunity for people to display their merit. Adversity builds strength, resolve, and creativity.

Okra is a heat-loving annual that is very productive. It does well in the south and is a staple of the southern diet. Okra is an ornamental plant ranging in size from 3 feet to over 6 feet tall. It is easy to grow and has a beautiful flower that makes it very captivating. Okra's long slender shape has given it the nickname "lady's fingers."

When harvesting okra, look for fully developed pods but not seed ready. Big pods are rubbery and difficult to eat. New pods will grow until the first frost. Okra is a superb side dish, and it is a beautiful ingredient for many different dishes.

History

Okra originated in Ethiopia (Abyssinia region). From there, it made its way to the ancient Egyptians around the 12th century B.C. From Egypt, its popularity and cultivation expanded throughout North Africa and eventually to the Middle East.

The ancient world boiled, roasted, basted, and baked okra. Okra made its way to the Caribbean and the U.S. in the 1700s via slaves from West Africa. After arriving in America, okra made its way to Western Europe.

The rural poor and African Americans were the first users of okra. During the 1900s, as people moved to the city and became more prosperous, people's negative perception of okra reduced consumption. For okra, the early to mid-1900s was a challenging time. Okra got a reputation for being a poor person's food, an uneducated person's food, or a backwoods person's food.

That view is evolving. Okra is making a comeback! Southern food, Cajun cooking, and locally grown are working together to build an okra revival. People all across America are requesting okra at restaurants, markets, and farm stands, and you should provide it to them.

Competitive Advantage

Okra creates opportunities for cross-merchandising and marketing. Grocery stores are reporting skyrocketing okra sales, and there has been an 18% increase over the past three years. Recently, food lovers and chefs alike have discovered the versatility of okra.

Okra's abundance makes it great from a production standpoint. Okra is a very prolific crop. Just a few plants produce excellent yields. Okra's rise in popularity makes it great from a marketing standpoint. Any small farmer should grow this win-win product — okra pairs well with tomatoes, onions, and peppers, among other vegetables. *Growing okra allows small farmers to focus on a crop that has low inputs and high outputs.*

Marketing and Sales Strategies

When marketing okra, focus on its taste and health benefits. The best marketing strategy for okra is to focus on its many uses and ways to cook it. Prepare recipes and samples for fried okra, grilled okra pods, gumbos, and soups.

To help okra jump into shopping baskets, package okra in one-pound packages. This merchandising speeds up transaction time, makes it easier for customers to carry, and looks professional. These packages should be ready for the customer to put in their refrigerators. To increase value, attach a recipe card to each one highlighting okra's usefulness and versatility.

Production and growing

- **Soil and pH** - Okra grows best in well-composted soil with a near-neutral pH between 6.5 and 7.0. It will do fine in a pH as high as 7.6.
- **Nutrients** - Okra needs nitrogen (N) and phosphorus (P) at or before planting.
- **Water** - Okra needs a steady water supply. However, the irrigation should not be heavy because it may cool the soil and slow production. It is often best to water okra during the heat of the day.
- **Spacing** - Sow okra seeds ½ to 1 inch deep set 6 inches apart. Space rows 24 to 36 inches apart, and then thin sprouts 12 to 18 inches apart.
- **Growing Temp** - Soil temperature needs to be at least 65 degrees. It is rarely too hot for okra.
- **Pests** - Flea beetles and aphids may attack okra. Pinch out aphid-infested vegetation or knock flea beetles and aphids off plants with a strong stream of water.
- **Disease** - Okra is susceptible to verticillium and fusarium wilt that will cause plants to suddenly wilt, dry up, and die, usually in midsummer just as plants begin to produce.
- **Hardiness Zones** - Okra can be grown anywhere in America. The time of planting will depend on the last frost.
- **Tips** – Start okra indoors using peat pots under full light 3 to 4 weeks before the last frost date. Also, be sure to transplant the entire pod. Okra roots are

sensitive and do not like to be touched. Soak seed in warm water overnight to speed germination. Eliminate weeds when the plants are young, then mulch heavily to prevent more weeds from growing.

- **Harvest** – Harvest okra pods while still tender and before the seeds are half-grown. Typically 5 to 6 days after flowering. Pods with tips that will bend between the fingers without breaking are too harsh for use as fresh fruit. Most customers like okra pods to be around 2.5 to 3.5 inches long. To keep a steady supply, harvest it daily. When storing okra, do not wash it because it will become slimily.

Companion Plants

Okra gets along well with the following plants: basil, cucumbers, peppers, eggplant, melons, and southern peas. Basil helps with pest control, especially with aphids.

Eggplant and okra release nutrients that are beneficial to the other plant. Here is why. Okra puts nitrogen into the soil, a benefit to eggplant. Eggplant puts potassium into the ground, a gift to okra. Eggplants keep away harmful sap-sucking insects that often plague okra plants. Both okra and eggplant thrive in warm, regularly watered soil.

Melons benefit from okra's nitrogen release and grow quicker when planted next to okra. Melons benefit from okra's shade, and okra deters pests such as the cucumber beetles while attracting pollinating bees and butterflies. Melons and okra both prosper in warm soil.

Uses

Okra's primary use is as a side dish. Okra is a garnish for main dishes and drinks such as Bloody Marys. The flower is very decorative and is often used as a garnish or put in a flower bouquet. Okra plays well with foods with acidic flavors such as tomatoes, lemon juice, collard greens. A trend is to cook it with mango-inspired dishes. Okra provides the perfect balance for foods that have an earthy and woody flavor.

Okra also has many health benefits. Just one cup of okra has 30 calories, 3 grams of dietary fiber, 2 grams of protein, 7 grams carbohydrates, 0.1 grams of fat, 21 milligrams of vitamin C, around 88 micrograms of folate, and 57 milligrams of magnesium.

Okra can reduce asthma symptoms. Okra is high in soluble fiber, making it great for digestive health. Okra reduces bad cholesterol and is a good source of antioxidants, providing a boost against unsafe free radicals while boosting the immune system. Okra is also a good source of vitamin A and B, making it an excellent choice for pregnant women.

Fun Facts

- Cut okra pods ooze a mucilaginous juice that is an excellent thickener for stews, soups, and especially Gumbo. A much healthier option than corn starch.
- Okra is a good source of vitamins, iron, and calcium.
- Okra is a good source of dietary fiber and is fat-free.
- Okra is a tropical plant that grows best in warm climates.
- Quimbombo is another word for okra and okra-inspired dishes.
- Okra is related to cotton, and both are members of the mallow family of plants.
- The state meal of Oklahoma has okra in it.
- Young okra leaves can replace spinach or greens.
- Roasted Okra seeds can make a coffee-like drink.
- Okra is usable for rope production.
- The longest recorded okra pod was 18 inches long.
- The tallest recorded okra plant was just over 19 feet tall.
- "Fighting Okra Records" is a student-run record label at Delta State University in Cleveland, Mississippi.

Selected Varieties

Alabama Red Okra is a southern heirloom from Alabama. It grows up 7 feet tall and produces plump red-and-green pods. The red stems and leaves work to make this an attractive plant. This traditional okra is scrumptiously fried and injects color and piquancy to salads.

Beck's Big Buck Okra is an old German heirloom that grows 7 to 8 feet tall. This plant produces a vast bounty of large, hefty, and fork-tender pods. When young, these pods easily snap off the plant. This okra grows exceptionally well in Texas.

Bowling Red Okra is an American heirloom grown by the Bowling family during the early part of the 1900s. This plant grows up to 8 feet tall with red stalks and red pods. This okra is popular because the pods stay tender longer than most other varieties.

Burmese Okra is a Burma heirloom. This okra produces large, tender, spineless, and finely flavored pods. These pods will be an attractive creamy yellow as they mature. This variety starts making early and produces until frost.

Clemson Spineless Okra is an heirloom released by Clemson University in 1930. It is a spineless, 4-foot tall plant perfect for picking. This variety is popular with many gardeners and growers alike. It is easy to grow and tastes great.

Okra Eagle Pass is a Texas heirloom that is great in gumbo and stews. It is low maintenance, highly productive, and very tall (12 feet high).

Egyptian Okra is an old heirloom from Upper Egypt. This very productive okra grows 6-foot plants that can produce as many as 23 to 25 pods each. This okra is prolific right up to frost. The average pod length is 6 to 8 inches when mature, but 3 or 4 inches produces fork-tender pods. It tolerates droughts and production increases as the heat increases.

Fife Creek Cowhorn Okra is an heirloom that has been in the Fife family since 1900. The Fife family got this okra from a Creek Indian woman who stayed with them in Jackson, Mississippi, over 100 years ago. This plant produces long pods that stay tender. This plant is enormous at up to 12 feet in height and very productive.

Hill Country Orka is an heirloom plant from Texas. This okra is very drought and hot-weather-resistant. It produces pods that are up to 6 inches on plants that are 6 feet tall. It is a pickling okra, and pickled okra is a great value-added product. These pods are green with a red tip.

Jing Orange Okra is an ancient Asian heirloom with a charming plant and pod. This okra is tender even when the pods are 6 inches long. The stalks are scarlet red, and so are the pods. It is a very productive okra variety. This okra will brighten up displays and help move other products.

Mayan Okra is an heirloom from Belize in Central America. This okra plant has red stalks and does well in the heat. The pods are green and flavorful, and this okra is especially suited for gumbo and stews.

Star of David Okra is an heirloom from Israel. This longstanding variety produces short, thick pods that are perfect for stews, roasting, or gumbo. The leaves of this plant have purple streaks. This plant grows 6 to 10 feet high. Slicing this okra produces a star shape. This very productive plant can produce two pounds of pods for each plant.

Stelly Okra is an heirloom from Cajun country. This variety originates from St. Landry Parish, Louisiana, where it fended for itself at an old, abandoned homestead. Then in the 1950s, the new homestead owners saved this seed and plant. Since then, it has been growing in popularity. It is first-rate for gumbo and frying. It is easy to work with because the plants are only 5 to 6 feet tall and extremely productive. These pods are tender even when they are 6 to 7 inches long.

Onions

*"The onion and its satin wrappings is among the most beautiful of vegetables and is the only one that represents the essence of things. It can be said to have a soul." ~**Charles Dudley Warner***

Onions provide one of life's great metaphors. People are like an onion. Society is like an onion. Culture is like an onion. Knowledge is like an onion. As a matter of fact, anything with layers is like an onion. To fully understand anything in the proceeding list requires peeling away at the layers.

Onions are nature's reminder that things are not always straightforward. Many things that appear simple on the surface are complex below the surface. Onions by themselves are pungent and even repulsive; however, when combined with other items, onions are pleasant, attractive, and mouthwatering.

Onions are biennial plants planted in the spring for a fall harvest. When left in the ground, the onions will produce a flower and seeds during the second year.

Onions are edible anytime but are fully mature when the tops fall over. To harvest, gently pull the bulb and allow it to dry slowly in a well-ventilated, dark place for several weeks.

Daylight requirements determine onion classification. The three categories are short, intermediate, and long day onions.

Short-day onions require a minimum of 10 hours of daylight for proper growth. Known as southern onions, these are very sweet. Short-day onions do not store well.

Intermediate onions require 10 - 14 hours of daylight for proper growth. These onions do well in all regions. Intermediate onions are the most versatile onions and come in all shapes, sizes, and flavors.

Long-day onions require 14 hours of daylight for proper growth. These northern onions are low in sugar and are not as sweet. These onions do well when dried and have great storability.

History

Humans have been eating onions since before recorded history. Onion researchers have two schools of thought on their origins. One school claims that onions originated in central Asia. In contrast, the other school of thought argues that onions originated in Iran and West Pakistan.

Onions are one of the earliest cultivated crops because they were less perishable than other foods, transportable, easy to grow, and adapted to various soils and climates.

Here is some fascinating onion history. Since the beginning of recorded history, the Chinese have been growing onions, and Egyptians used them as far back as 3500 B.C. Also, the Sumerians used onions as far back as 2,500 BC. So, as you can see, onions have a widespread and ancient past.

The Romans ate onions regularly and carried them on journeys to their provinces in England and German, giving Europe onion access. Europeans started growing onions, and they became popular during the Middle Ages.

Onions have had many uses through the ages. Onions have been used to alleviate headaches, snakebites, and hair loss; they were often used for bartering and wedding gifts.

Competitive Advantage

Per capita, onion consumption has risen over 70 percent in the last two decades, from 12.2 pounds per person to 20 pounds per year. Onions are in over 70% of all households. Offering onions is a great way to move other products. Onions go great with many other vegetables such as tomatoes, peppers, potatoes, squash, etc.

Most onions in the store are the products of large-scale commercial growers. Consumers are continually looking for new local products. Growing onions offers people a local choice for this popular food.

Onions come in many different colors. To grab people's attention, grow purple or red onions. These onions are more expensive at the retail level and attractive on the stand.

Marketing and Sales Strategies

Onions have multiple uses, so cross-merchandise them with everything from meat to salad. Any marketing program with onions must include hamburgers and steaks, green peppers, soup supplies, stir-fry vegetables, and bagged salads.

Promote onions as a grilling option and topping for burgers, hotdogs, or other grilled items. Promote onions as a soup onion by underscoring the flavor and texture onions bring to the table. Promote onions as an Asian cuisine by providing stir-fry recipes. Onions excel as a grilled meat topping. Red, white and yellow onions juxtapose color and attract customers.

Production and growing

- **Soil and pH** - Onions do best with loose soil with organic matter that allows for easy expansion of the bulb. Optimal onion pH is 5.5 - 6.5, favoring a more slightly acidic side.
- **Nutrients** - Onions require nitrogen (N) and need a steady diet of nitrogen throughout the growing season. Sulphur (S) promotes the formation of leaves and bulbs during the early stages of growth and aids in onion formation. Phosphorus (P) for root development. Potassium (K) promotes the growth of the roots and the leaves while increasing foliar activity for proper bulb

development and aids with water absorption while protecting diseases.

- **Water** - Onions require at least an inch of water a week. The goal is to keep the soil moist so it will not dry out.
- **Spacing** - When growing in rows, onions should be 4 to 5 inches apart, with rows spaced 12 to 18 inches. If growing in beds, onions should be 6 to 8 inches apart in all directions.
- **Growing Temp** – Plant onions while the temperatures are above 20 degrees. Leaf, root, and bulb development occurs during temperatures between 55° to 75°F. Ideal leaf growth occurs at 68° to 77°F. When forming bulbs, onions easily tolerate temperatures higher than 75°F.
- **Pests** - Onions are susceptible to thrips, which will cut the epidermis, stems, or leaves to feed on the sap. Also, onions attract the onion fly, lay eggs that grow into larvae that feed between the leaves and small bulbs or roots. Cutworms will climb the onion stem and eat/bore tiny holes into the stem. Lastly, the armyworm loves the taste of the onion shafts and leaves.
- **Disease** - Common onion diseases include downy mildew. Pink root is also common with onions, and symptoms include dying leaves that turn pink to red to yellow. Pink root is a soil-borne fungus occurring in wet soil.
- **Hardiness Zones** - Sunlight is the most crucial planting factor. Short-day onions do well in southern zones 7 – 11. Long day onions do well in northern zones 1 – 6. Intermediate onions do well anywhere.

- **Tips** - Onions must be kept dry and at room temperature. Wet onions will spoil quickly, so keep them away from water-misters and refrigeration. Plant onions in full sun. When planting onions, add nitrogen and keep adding nitrogen every few weeks. Using mulch will retain moisture and suppress weeds in onion patches. Pungent onions will store longer than sweet onions.
- **Harvest** – To harvest the onions, wait for the tops to yellow and fall over. Loosen the soil to start the drying process. Once the tops are brown, pull the onions. It is usually late summer, before cool weather. Mature onions will spoil in fall weather.

Companion Plants

Onions work well with cabbage. Onions deter cabbage-loving pests such as cabbage loopers, worms, and maggots. Onions need full sun, and cabbage is a spring or fall crop that is low to the ground making for a great partnership.

Onions play well with many other plants because the strong smell of onions tends to overpower and hide other plants' smell. Other low-growing options to consider: beets, brassicas, carrots, kohlrabi, leeks, lettuce, and strawberries.

Some people claim onions are companions for tomatoes and dill. This one-way relationship does not benefit onions. These plants will put onions in the shade. Also, onions do not mix with asparagus, beans, or peas.

Uses

Onions contain quercetin, a cataract, heart disease, and cancer-preventing antioxidant. Onions also prevent bone-density loss and help prevent osteoporosis. Onions are a good source of Vitamin C, and research shows onions have anti-inflammatory benefits.

Onions are typically a great ingredient, side dish, or appetizer. The type of onion determines its use. For example, yellow onions are universal; unless a recipe calls for a specific onion, use yellow onions.

Sweet onions are bigger and flatter than yellow onions and are lighter in color. Sweet onions have more carbs, making them perfect for grilling. The sugar caramelizes and adds a great taste and texture to most dishes. Sweet onions are the go-to onions for onion rings or onion blossoms.

White onions have a wispy white exterior with a milder and sweeter taste than yellow onions. White onions are great for serving raw in fresh salsa or homemade guacamole.

Red or purple onions have a deep, magenta color, which makes them particularly good for salads or anywhere. A splash of color always enhances any dish's appearance, and colorful onions add color, flavor, and nutrients.

Shallots are small, brown-skinned onions with purplish flesh. Green onions are immature onions that have not yet formed a bulb or only partially formed. Green onions make an excellent garnish or add-in for soups, breads, omelets, and tacos, providing color and crunch.

Fun Facts

- In Egypt, onions were an object of worship.
- The Egyptians saw eternal life in the anatomy of the onion because of its circle-within-a-circle structure.
- King Ramses IV had onions entombed in his eye sockets.
- Pedanius Dioscorides, a Greek physician, noted several medicinal uses of onions.
- Annually farmers raise one hundred five billion pounds of onions.
- Refrigerating onions for 30 minutes reduces tears when cutting.
- To loosen the onion peel, run under warm water.
- Southport, Connecticut, is the Onion Capital of North America.
- The fastest time to eat a raw onion is 29.56 seconds, achieved by Yusuke Yamaguch.
- An urban myth states that sliced onions become poisonous.
- The world record for the heaviest onion is 18 pounds 11.84 ounces.
- The world record for eating onion rings is 6.73 pounds in 8 Minutes.
- Ancient English folklore states thick-skinned onions predict a hard winter. Thin skin onions predict a mild winter.
- New York City was the Big Onion before it was the Big Apple.
- In ancient times, onions treated wartime wounds.

- Onions prevented scurvy during long ocean voyages.
- The average American eats almost 20 pounds of onions annually.
- Pace Foods uses 21 million pounds of fresh onions every year.
- The official state vegetable of Georgia is the Vidalia onion.
- The official state vegetable of Texas is the Texas Sweet onion.
- Sliced onion can soothe insect bites and burns on the skin.
- Onions combined with crushed aspirin and water are a folk treatment to cure warts.
- Libya has the highest consumption of onions, with an astounding average per capita consumption of 66.8 pounds.
- Onions represent the third largest fresh vegetable industry in the United States.

Selected Varieties

Ailsa Craig Onion is a long day heirloom from Scotland with massive staying power. It has been popular since the late 1880s; this giant onion weighing up to 5 pounds is a sweet, mild-tasting yellow onion. This onion does not store well. The Ailsa Craig has a lower water content making it an excellent choice for frying.

Australian Brown Onion is an intermediate day heirloom from the land down under. It produces bulbs with a strong, pungent flavor and is a good choice for most culinary applications. This onion has above-average storability.

Bermuda Onion is a short day heirloom. A small onion great for stuffing chicken, turkey, duck, or other protein products. This onion is an excellent feature for casseroles and other baking dishes. These onions are sweet and unassuming when mixed in with other ingredients. These onions originated from the island of Bermuda.

Bianca Di Guino Onion is a short day heirloom. A slow to mature cippolini onion, these small flat onions are great for pickling, roasting, and grilling. It is an outstanding choice for Italian food.

Brunswick Onion is a long-day German heirloom that has a purple color and a flat shape. It has a sweet, mild taste that is a natural choice for traditional German fare. First offered commercially in 1870, it has been popular for a very long time. This sweet onion has exceptional storability.

Common Chives is an "any day" heirloom because they do well with very little daylight and are easy to grow in most areas. Chives are native to Europe and Asia. Many of the modern and heirloom onions are descendants of the common chive.

Garlic Chives are an "any day" variety heirloom. Also known as Chinese chives. This onion has a slim, flat grass-like leaf that tastes likes a combination of sweet garlic and common chives. The flowers of this plant are white and edible.

Flat of Italy Onion is an Intermediate day heirloom. This heirloom is a red Cipollini-style onion that has a flat shape. This onion is a smart option for eating fresh or cooking. This onion's roots go back to 1885 in Italy, a steller choice for farmers markets and farm stands.

He-Shi Ko Bunching Onion is a short day heirloom from Asia. A non-bulb-forming bunching onion, the stalks are mild and delicious. This onion does incredibly well in stir-fry dishes—a fantastic seller in markets with an Asian presence.

Ishikura Onion is a short-day Japanese heirloom perfect for bunching. The most common use is like a chive because it is a non-bulb-forming onion with long white stalks. Most people use this like a chive. The mild taste of this heirloom gives any dish an Asian-infused flavor.

Jaune Paille Des Vertus Onion is an easy-to-grow long day heirloom. This onion was widespread in Europe during the early 1900s. This rather large onion grows to 3-inches in diameter. The flat bottom makes this onion a great displayer.

The exterior of this onion is yellow, and the interior is white to pale green.

Mattamuskeet Sweet Onion is an intermediate day heirloom from North Carolina. This onion is extremely popular in Eastern North Carolina. It is an excellent choice for cooking and is very rare outside of North Carolina. For growers on the same latitude as North Carolina, this rare and proven onion is a perfect choice for growing.

Mayan Sweet Onion is a short day heirloom. This onion is a first cousin to the Vidalia onion. This onion has many of the same characteristics as the Vidalia onion, including wall thickness, sweetness, and an overall flat profile. It requires low sulfur soil. This onion comes to North America from Peru, where it has been popular for years.

Noordhollandse Bloedrode Onion is a long day heirloom, often referred to as Dutch Red. These onions are large, bright red, shiny, and delicious. This onion has a spicy taste and is a great keeper. When small, these onions make magnificent scallions; this is a great grower in the north, but not so much in the south.

Red Creole Onion is a short day heirloom. As the name implies, this an extraordinary cooking onion for the south. This onion's spicy taste and red flesh are an alluring add-in to gumbos, soups, or other dishes. This onion stores for months. The Red Creole was a standard crop onion in

Louisiana until the 1850s. This onion requires a growing season of 200 days.

Redwing Onion is a long day dark read heirloom with a mild flavor. It is a standard sandwich onion. The redwing is very popular in the areas where it is grown. This onion is consistent, has thick skin, and stores well. The flesh of this onion will continue to darken during storage. For many growers, this onion is a standard item.

Round Tropea Onion is an intermediate day heirloom. This heirloom is viral in Italy, where the locals refer it to as the Cipolla di Tropea. This Minoan-era onion arrived in Italy through trade with the Greeks. It is a lovely purple onion that has a round and elongated shape with a sweet taste. This onion could make a value-added Italian marmalade.

Southport Red Globe is a medium-sized long-day heirloom released by D. M. Ferry Seeds in 1873. It is one of the best-tasting and best-yielding purple onions and a great storing red onion varieties with excellent resistance to fusarium rot.

Southport White Globe Onion is a long-day heirloom with two aliases, "Silver Ball" or "White Rocca." Named from the Connecticut town of Southport, this is a large onion with a mild flavor. This onion has great storability and transports well.

Spanish Onion is in an intermediate-day heirloom requiring 14 hours of sunlight. It is sweeter than most yellow onions because of its lower water content. Its reduced water content makes it perfect for frying or stuffing, which is why foodservice customers adore it. It is the most popular onion in the United States. It is easily recognizable because of its round shape and thick brown skin.

Stuttgarter Onion is a long day heirloom; it is a delicious medium-sized yellow onion that stores well. Typically, it is a fall planting onion. This onion is very popular in the north and is ready in just 80 days. This onion is slow to bolt during unfavorable conditions and produces very high yields.

Tokyo Long White is a short day heirloom from Japan that can grow anywhere in the United States. This Japanese bunching-style onion is long and slender. It has a sweet and mild taste that goes great with Japanese dishes.

Tropea Lunga Onion is a short-day heirloom from southern Italy; it is a long slender purple onion thick in the middle with tapered ends. It is a great grilling onion. The color and shape of this onion allow it to be stacked high for an attractive display.

Violet de Galmi Onion is a short-day heirloom from the Ader Valley of Southeast Niger. Its thick pinkish-purple bulb is majestic raw or cooked. It is a famous onion in most of Africa, gaining popularity in the United States. The Violet de Galmi has above-average storability and makes for a unique offering at any farmer's market. A hardy and slow-maturing onion that takes 130 - 150 days to mature.

Wethersfield Red Onion is a long day heirloom from Connecticut. First marketed as "large red," this onion has a large red oblate shape with a strong flavor. The Wethersfield can reach up to 8 inches in diameter. It is a good choice for pickling and was one of the most popular pickling onions during the late 1800s. It has above-average storability.

Welsh Onions is a short-day Chinese heirloom. It is a bunching onion with a chive-like flavor. Perfect for stir-fry and Asian fusion dishes. The Welsh are a very easy onion to grow, and they can be stacked high, making a great display.

Yellow Flat Dutch Onion is a long day heirloom from Germany brought to America in 1888 by the RH Allen Co. It is easy to grow, large in size, and stores well. Its mild flavor makes it a popular customer choice.

Peppers

We got married in a fever -- hotter than a pepper sprout.
~June Carter Cash

Peppers are nature's metaphors. For example, Chili peppers symbolize warmth and friendship. Sweet peppers symbolize health and prosperity. Jalapeno peppers symbolize what may be fun today but can burn you tomorrow.

Peppers have many different meanings and uses. There is a pepper for any mood, feeling, or situation. Peppers are adaptable for any situation, and there is a pepper idiom to describe virtually any situation.

Peppers are annual plants harvest-ready in 60 days. Peppers are part of the capsicum genus, and the amount of capsaicin a pepper determines the amount of heat. The lower the capsaicin, the sweeter a pepper; the higher the capsaicin, the hotter a pepper. Peppers come in a variety of shapes, sizes, and colors. Peppers do well in warm climates but not too hot.

Peppers are popular with many different diets and can function as a main dish, side dish, or an ingredient - including drying for seasoning. People have eaten peppers for thousands of years.

Hot peppers have a cult following. There are hot pepper eating contests, festivals, and events. A recent social media trend was the "hot pepper challenge" that featured a person recording their reaction to eating a hot pepper – something that will trend again.

Peppers deserve their own book. This book will focus on a few heirlooms that do well in most markets. The wide variety of peppers provide growers an opportunity for something distinctive.

History

Ancient Americans began using wild peppers and chilies as soon as they arrived in South America. These people mixed peppers with other foods and stored them by drying them. Selective breeding gave rise to modern peppers around 6,000 years ago. More varieties developed after Columbus brought peppers to Spain.

Columbus brought peppers from the Taino people of Bermuda, who called peppers "aji." From Spain, peppers spread to Africa, India, Asia, and eventually the rest of Europe.

Peppers did not make it to the colonies until the 1600s. Once here, it took 300 years for peppers to join mainstream acceptance and earn designation as a culinary asset. *Currently, the average American eats 6 pounds of peppers annually, making it one of the most popular vegetables.*

Competitive Advantage

Peppers are a billion-dollar business that continues to expand. Last year 54% of consumers purchased bell peppers.

It is an excellent opportunity for heirloom growers. Most grocery stores carry fewer than ten types of peppers. Heirloom growers can grow peppers not offered in retail stores, and growers have many different options to market those peppers.

Some growers sell small mini-peppers in convenient one-pound packages that are easy to store and carry. Other growers create products such as roasted red peppers, peppers preserved in oil, pickled peppers, or pepper jelly.

Peppers have year-round demand making them an excellent option for hoop or greenhouses. Peppers are easy to propagate by cloning, thus reducing planting costs and speeding up production.

Marketing and Sales Strategies

Peppers are a versatile product that goes great with most other products such as greens, salads, onions, etc. During the spring, peppers are great for salads and fresh use. During the summer, peppers are great for grilling and a healthy snack while traveling. In the fall, they pack well in lunch boxes. In the winter, they are great stuff or roasted.

Peppers make a great item for customers to sample by providing a dipping such as ranch or hummus. When talking about peppers, be sure to talk up their health and cancer-fighting qualities. Peppers fight infection while boosting the immune system. Many peppers contain vitamin A, B6, and C.

The kaleidoscope of pepper colors creates a vibrant display. Green, red, orange, and purple peppers are captivating. A proper pepper display gets people to stop and to purchase from your stand.

When stacking peppers, do not stack them more than two or three high. Consider building a pyramid display that will give peppers a taller display. Packaging peppers in tray packs makes them easier to handle and price while speeding up transaction time. When packaging peppers, include three or four peppers of different colors in the package. It allows customers to experience multiple types of peppers.

Valued added products for peppers include roasted peppers in snack-sized bags. Dried whole peppers or ground peppers for seasonings are more value-added ideas. Jellies, jams, and marmalade made with peppers are always a hit. Peppers are an excellent pickling item or great ingredients in other pickled products. Hot sauce is a popular value-added item. Locally sourced hot sauce is a great way to build your brand.

Production and growing

- **Soil and pH** - Peppers have shallow roots and grow well in loose, heavy with lots of organic material that drains easily. Optimal pepper pH is between 6.5 and 7.0.
- **Nutrients** - Peppers need nitrogen (N), phosphorus (P), and potassium(K), along with trace minerals such as magnesium for healthy growth and fruit. The most popular fertilizer is a 20-20-20 blend.

- **Water** - Peppers develop a shallow root system and need watering once or twice a week depending on soil type and rainfall. Peppers need about one inch of water per week. Peppers especially need water during flowering and fruit onset to prevent the shedding of flowers and small fruits.
- **Spacing** – Plant peppers in single or twin rows on a raised bed. Double rows increase plant populations and marketable yields. Peppers are spaced 12 to 24 inches between plants, with each row or bed 4 to 5 feet in the center. In double rows, peppers need to be spaced 18 inches apart on the bed using a herringbone pattern.
- **Growing Temp** – Start peppers 2 to 4 weeks before the last frost. Peppers germinate when the temperature is 70 to 75 degrees. The ideal growth occurs when the weather is 80 to 85 degrees.
- **Pests** - Insects that like peppers include the European corn borer, pepper maggot, aphids, thrips, stinkbugs, spider mites, and cucumber beetle.
- **Disease** - Several diseases can attack peppers, including bacterial leaf spot, phytophthora blight, anthracnose, and viruses.
- **Hardiness Zones** - Peppers can grow almost anywhere in North America but do best in zones 9 through 11
- **Tips** – Peppers are slow to germinate and do better when transplanted. One ounce of pepper seeds produces 1,500 to 2,000 transplants. High tunnels and solar-heated greenhouses extend the pepper growing season.

- **Harvest** – Harvest peppers when they reach the desired size and color. Larger and colorful peppers are more valuable. However, they take longer to harvest. A good yield of peppers is 700 to 800 bushels per acre.

Companion Plants

Peppers are friendly. Peppers enjoy the opportunity to share space with many other plants. Herbs and peppers are great friends and do well as roommates. Basil repels insects such as thrips, flies, and mosquitoes. Parsley is an excellent wasp and pollinator attractor. Dill attracts beneficial insects while repelling pests.

Vegetables that play well with peppers include spinach, lettuce, and chard. These plants will crowd out weeds while being ready for harvest before it is time to pick peppers. It is beneficial for urban growers who need to maximize garden space and get in an additional crop. Beets and parsnips can also fill in space and keep weeds at bay while keeping the soil cool and moist.

Corn serves as a windbreak and sun barrier to peppers. At the same time, beans and peas fix nitrogen into the soil, a necessary nutrient for peppers. Buckwheat is a pollinator attractant and, when harvested, serves as mulch for the garden.

Uses

Peppers are immensely popular as an adaptable food.
People stuff peppers for a main dish or as an appetizer.
People roast, grill, or fry peppers as a side dish. People slice,
dice, or mince peppers as an ingredient for other meals.
People slice peppers as toppings for salads, hamburgers, and
sandwiches. People dice peppers for nachos, omelets, and
quiches. Lastly, people dry and ground peppers for flavor in
all types of sauces or spices.

Peppers have medicinal uses. Capsaicin fights infections by
rushing blood to areas where it is applied. Capsaicin is a
topical analgesic that numbs the skin.

Hot peppers are used for self-defense. Pepper spray causes
breathing difficulties, runny nose, pain in the eyes, and
temporary blindness. Peppers are also used as an organic
pest and wild animal repellent.

Fun Facts

- Capsaicin is a chemical produced in peppers that sets off
  heat-detecting sensors in the brain.
- The Scoville scale measures pepper heat. The more
  capsaicin, the hotter the food.
- On the Scoville scale, the hottest pepper is the Carolina
  Reaper with Scoville heat units of 1,400,000-2,200,000. In
  contrast, the standard Jalapeno pepper measures in at
  2,500 – 8,000, and the Bell pepper comes in at zero.

- Aztecs would punish children by holding them over chili pepper smoke.
- Within 50 years of Columbus' voyages, peppers made it to India, Japan, and China.
- Peppers made it to the American Colonies with the English in 1621.
- Bolivia is the chili pepper birthplace and is home to dozens of wild species.
- Chili pepper extracts thwart many microbial pathogens.
- Many topical pain relievers use capsaicin.
- Red peppers contain lycopene, which lowers the risk of certain types of cancer.
- The "chili" in chili pepper is from Nahuatl, an Aztec language.
- Immature or green peppers contain lutein.
- Yellow chili peppers contain violaxanthin, a beneficial carotenoid.
- Peppers contain ferulic acid, a compound useful in the battle against diabetes.
- The jalapeno pepper was the first pepper in space.

Selected Varieties

Aji Amarillo is a hot pepper with a 40,000 to 50,000 Scoville rating. It is one of the most popular and critical Peruvian heirlooms. A yellow chili pepper is used raw, grilled, roasted, dried, or ground into powder. This pepper is best when it is 3 to 5 inches long. It is the perfect choice for making Peruvian hot sauce or using it in South American meals.

Aji Cito is a hot pepper with a 100,000 Scoville rating. An heirloom from Peru that is torpedo shape and is as wide as a person's hand. When the Aji Cito is fully mature, it turns a dazzling orange. It makes a flavorful choice for salads, meals, or dried and powdered. It is an excellent item for a volcano-level hot sauce.

Aji Limo is a hot pepper with a 30,000 to 50,000 Scoville rating. This Peruvian heirloom is 2 to 3 inches long that comes in a rainbow of colors, including red, yellow, orange, purple, or white. It is a pre-Columbian pepper with a hint of citrus. This plant is 18 inches tall and is more cold tolerant than other pepper plants.

Aji Pineapple has moderate heat with a 10,000 to 20,000 Scoville rating. It is a beautiful yellow pepper from Peru with 2 to 3-inch elongated fruits. This pepper has a slightly fruity taste that flatters the heat. This pepper is virtually impossible to find outside of Peru. A great pepper for growers that want something truly unique.

Aji Panca is a sweet pepper with a low 1,000 to 1,500 Scoville rating. It is one of the most popular peppers in the Andes. This pepper is a deep red to burgundy pepper that ranges from 3 to 5 inches in size. This pepper grows best near the coast and can withstand cooler nighttime temperatures. The Aji Panca pepper has a mildly sweet, berry-like taste with a delicate smoky essence.

Aji Habanero – The Aji Habanero is a mild pepper with a 5,000 to 10,000 Scoville rating. This pepper has only a fraction of the heat of a regular habanero. It does have a similar taste and flavor. It is an outstanding choice for people that like the habanero flavor but not the heat. This very marketable pepper makes a tremendous value-added mild habanero hot sauce.

Aju Charapita is a hot pepper with a 30,000 to 50,000 Scoville rating. It is a rare pepper in the States; however, it is one of the most wanted and exclusive peppers in Peru. This pepper grows wild—a highly productive plant producing 100s of small round yellow berry-like peppers hot when mature.

Ajvarski Sweet Pepper is a mild pepper with a 500 - 4,000 Scoville rating. This pepper is from eastern Macedonia. This plant grows about two feet tall, produces fruits that are 6 - 7 inches wide, and turns red as it matures. It is a thick flesh pepper that is an excellent roaster or stuffer. In Macedonia, natives use this pepper to make a relish called ajvar. For growers looking for a unique value-added item, ajvar relish is a great idea.

Anaheim Peppers is a mild pepper with a 5,000 Scoville rating that is 6 to 10 inches long and 1 to 2 inches wide. Anaheim peppers come in a variety of colors. These peppers are delicious when dried. These peppers add heat and flavor to dishes without overpowering other ingredients.

Banana Peppers is a sweet to mild pepper with a 500 Scoville rating. These peppers become sweeter as they mature. Banana peppers are juicy, tang, sweet, and have a classic pepper taste without the heat. A beneficial pepper that adds flavor to salads, salsa, sandwiches, or it can become a main course when stuffed.

Bullnose Peppers is a very mild pepper with a 0 - 100 Scoville rating. This pepper was grown at Monticello. This medium-sized bell pepper is excellent for salads or cooking. This pepper turns red as it matures and is a classic bell pepper.

Cayenne Pepper is a hot pepper with a 25,000 to 50,000 Scoville rating. It is a drying pepper typically ground into a seasoning. When fresh, this pepper is perfect for cooking or using raw. Cayenne peppers have the same uses as any other pepper. By grilling, pickling, and roasting this pepper, you are entering a culinary adventure.

Chocolate Seven Pot Hot Peppers is a scorching pepper with a 990,000 to over one million Scoville rating from Trinidad.   It is also called the 7 Pot Douglah because one pepper can season 7 pots. Buried by the hotness is a fruity and somewhat nutty tasting pepper. It is a YouTube hot pepper challenge favorite.

It is an attention hogging pepper, and the name of this pepper is a perfect name for salsa or hot sauce. It is excellent for sampling and creating pepper-eating challenges - just be sure people know what they are getting into!

Chocolate Beauty Pepper is a mild pepper with a 0-100 Scoville rating. A sizeable blocky bell pepper that turns chocolate brown as it matures. It is a very productive, heavily producing plant. It is an excellent variety for market growers because it produces quickly, produces several, and produces persistently.

Corne De Chevre is a hot pepper with a 225,000 - 300,000 Scoville rating. This pepper is a medium-sized pepper shaped like a goat's horn and is a favorite for hot sauce making.

Doux D'Espagne or Spanish Mammoth Pepper is a sweet and mild pepper with a 0 - 100 Scoville rating. First introduced in the early 1800s, this pepper is large and easy to grow. The fruits are 6 - 7 inches long and are great for stuffing, cooking, or eating raw. It is a good-producing pepper that is disease resistant and always a good seller.

Etiuda Pepper is a sweet pepper with zero heat. This pepper can be up to half a pound, and it turns orange as it ages; when mature this pepper maintains its crispness, sweetness, and juiciness. It is an excellent market pepper from Poland that grows well both in the ground and greenhouse. It is a good item for markets with a Polish influence.

Figitelli Sicilia is a sweet pepper with a 0 to 500 Scoville rating. This heirloom has a dense wall and crisp texture with a pepperoncino look. It is trendy in its home country of Italy, where it is pickled. This sweet pepper turns red as it matures and has just the slightest touch of heat. This pepper is a great market pepper that travels and displays well.

Golden Marconi Pepper is a sweet pepper with a 0 to 100 Scoville rating – an Italian heirloom that produces yellow fruits up to 7 inches long. For Italian dishes, it is fried and served with marinara on a bed of pasta. The size and shape of this pepper make it great for a farmers market and roadside stands.

Habanero Chili Pepper is a hot pepper with a 150,000 to 350,000 Scoville rating. This popular heirloom never goes out style. Habanero peppers are green, yellow, red, or pink. It is a smaller pepper that is only 1.5 inches long — Habanero pepper compliments fruits such as mango. Growers may want to consider making a branded garden-fresh mango/habanero salsa if growing these peppers.

Italian Long Pepper is a mild to hot pepper and has the broadest Scoville rating of any pepper. Often referred to as the Russian roulette of peppers because some are mild and some are very hot. In Italy, these peppers are typically fried. These heirlooms add great texture and heat to sandwiches or most Italian dishes. It is a great choice to cook with olive oil, parsley, salt, and black pepper, and then serve on a hard roll with a sharp cheese slice.

Italian Pepperoncini Pepper is a mild heirloom with a 100 to 500 Scoville rating. It is perfect for pickling and maybe the most popular pickling pepper. The fruits of this pepper grow to about 3 ½ inches long with thin walls.

It is a sweet pepper with slight heat. These peppers turn red as they mature, which makes them great for salads and sandwiches. Market growers can effortlessly turn these peppers into a value-added pickled product.

Jalapeno Peppers is a mild pepper with a 4,000 Scoville rating. It is one of the most popular peppers, and it comes in various forms. They come in colors such as purple, red, yellow, or black.

Jalapenos are picked when they reach 2 to 3 inches long. This pepper becomes sweeter as it ages. Jalapeno peppers are best when they are firm with smooth skin. Jalapenos prefer a more alkaline soil than other pepper varieties.

Kalocsai Pepper is a hot pepper with a 10,000 - 15,000 Scoville rating. The fruit of this pepper grows to be 6 ½" long by 1 ¼" wide. It is a red pepper when it matures. Grilling, roasting, and drying are great uses for this pepper. When dried, it becomes the main ingredient of Hungarian Paprika, a profitable value-added product.

Korean Hot Pepper is a hot pepper with a 10,000 - 20,000 Scoville rating. This pepper comes in a short or long variety. It is a very productive plant that produces peppers 1 inch long by ¾ inch wide.

The long variety produces peppers that are 4 ½ inches long and 3/4 inches wide. Both types of peppers are sizzling and turn red as they mature. This pepper is an indispensable ingredient in many Korean dishes.

Lemon Drop Pepper or Hot Lemon pepper is a somewhat hot pepper with a 15,000 to 30,000 Scoville rating. This Peruvian pepper is very rare outside of its home country. This pepper grows on a plant that looks more vine-like than other pepper plants. The fruit of this plant has very few seeds. This heirloom is 2.5 inches long with a crinkled cone shape. In Peru, this pepper is used fresh, smoked, or in salsa.

Mareko Fana Pepper is a mild to hot pepper with a 5,000 to 30,000 Scoville rating. A slow to mature plant that produces good yields of 3 inches long by ¾-inch wide hot peppers. These peppers turn from light green to brown as they grow. This Ethiopian pepper makes great salsa or sauces — a popular item for Ethiopian cuisine.

Mulato Isleno Pepper is a mild pepper with a 1,000 - 1,500 Scoville rating. This pepper is large and measures 6 inches long by 3 inches wide. This pepper turns brown as it matures and is an excellent stuffing pepper. This pepper is originally from Mexico, where it has been used for thousands of years in many traditional Mexican dishes.

Mushroom Hot Pepper is a hot pepper with a 10,000 - 15,000 Scoville Rating. This plant produces fruit that is 1 inch long by 1 ½ inch wide, giving it a mushroom appearance. This pepper turns to yellow or orange as it matures. It is a rare heirloom from the United States whose attractiveness makes a good choice for markets and farm stands.

Naga Jolokia Purple is a hot pepper with an 800,000 to 1,000,000 Scoville Rating. This northeastern Indian heirloom is one of the hottest peppers globally, and it requires heat and humidity to grow well. It is a slow-growing plant, but patience earns growers bragging rights for having the hottest pepper in the market.

Ostra-Cyklon Pepper is a mild pepper with a 1,000 - 1,500 on the Scoville scale. This pepper is from Poland, with thin walls that make for easy drying. It is a good grower because it has productive plants with high yields. The peppers are 4.5 inches long and 1.5 inches wide, with fruits that turn red as they mature. It is the critical ingredient in Polish paprika, which is a profitable value-added product.

Pasilla Bajio Pepper is a mild pepper with a 1,000 - 2,000 Scoville rating. This dark green pepper turns brown as it matures. It is the pepper used in mole sauce and is an attractive newcomer to the market. Make sure you highlight this pepper's role in mole sauce.

Pimiento De Padron Pepper is a mild pepper with a 500 to 2,500 Scoville rating. An unpredictable pepper is nicknamed the Spanish Roulette because of the occasional hot pepper. A Spanish heirloom, this plant produces bite-sized green fruits. This pepper is often sautéed in olive oil and served with coarse-ground sea salt.

Scotch Bonnet Pepper is a hot pepper with an 80,000 to 400,000 Scoville rating. In some areas, give it the name Caribbean red. These peppers are available in a wealth of colors. It is a renowned pepper for Jamaican dishes and is very popular in the Caribbean region.

Serrano Peppers is a hot pepper with a 10,000 - 23,000 Scoville rating and one of Mexico's most popular peppers. They are thin-skinned with meaty flesh and perfect for making Pico de Gallo. Serrano peppers have a jalapeno taste but with more heat.

Sheepnose Pimento Pepper is a sweet pepper with a 100 - 1,000 Scoville rating. This Ohio heirloom produces small fruit with a thick wall. When young, it is green turning red as it matures. This pepper is a very popular add-in for cheeses.

Shishito Pepper is a sweet pepper with a 50 to 100 Scoville rating. This Japanese heirloom produces 3" long crinkly fruits perfect for tempura or other traditional Japanese recipes. This pepper is green and turns red as it matures. It is an excellent item for growers considering tempura to their value-added line.

Syrian Three-Sided Pepper is a sweet pepper with a 1 to 1,000 Scoville rating. As the name implies, this pepper is from Syria. This plant produces enormous fruits about the size of a coffee cup. These fruits grow to about 6 to 8 inches long and change color from green to red as they mature. This pepper is a terrific stuffing pepper that is a consistent seller.

Thai Bird Chilies is a hot pepper with a 50,000 to 100,000 Scoville rating. It is popular in Africa and Southeast Asia because they are adaptable to many different culinary situations. They add just the right amount of spice to curry, soups, or other Vietnamese fares. It is a smart choice for markets with either African or Southeast Asian clients.

Topepo Giallo Sweet pepper is a mild pepper with a 1 - 1,000 Scoville rating. This Italian heirloom turns yellow when fully matured. A giant pepper great for stuffing, but it does well pickled. The size and color of this pepper make it superb for markets and roadside stands.

Wax Peppers is a medium-hot flavor with a 5,000 to 10,000 Scoville rating. Often mistaken for banana chilies, wax peppers liven up salads or salsas. This Hungarian heirloom is an excellent pickling pepper. This pepper is easy to grow and is always a good seller.

Potatoes

"The man who has nothing to boast of but his ancestors is like a potato – the only good belonging to him is underground."
~ **Sir Thomas Overbury**

Potatoes are one-half of the meat and potatoes equation. Potatoes focus on what is critical. They strip away the fluff. In a world that complicates things, potatoes moved forward by keeping things simple. Potatoes realize that just because something is important, it should not be complicated.

Potatoes have the initiative to grow in harsh climates. Potatoes are willing to better their situations regardless of natural hardships and ambiguous opportunities.

The potato is a popular perennial plant grown as an annual. People eat the tuber root portion of this nightshade plant, which provides protein, nutrients, vitamins, and plant propagation.

Potatoes are versatile. They perform as an ingredient, side dish, or main dish. They are the ultimate comfort food with more than 3,500 varieties of native potatoes and over 150 wild potatoes.

Potatoes can be brown, tan, yellow, red, blue, and purple. Potatoes grow best on cool nights. Potato classification is according to the number of days required for harvest: "early" season (75-90 days), "midseason" (90-135 days), and "late-season" (135-160 days).

History

Potatoes made their way into the human food chain in South America 10,000 years ago when they became a staple food source for the Incas. It allowed the Incas to focus on building the largest and most sophisticated civilization in Mesoamerica. The Incas built terraces, canals, and cisterns to grow potatoes as well as corn and quinoa. These foods were easily stored and carried, proving sustenance for their military as they conquered much of the western South American coast.

Conquistadors brought potatoes back to Europe in the 1500s; however, it was not until the 1600s that potatoes spread through Europe. The potato's popularity grew as people discovered the benefits, versatility, and taste. Potatoes were instrumental during the discovery age because they prevented scurvy while delivering essential nutrients to armies and sailors.

People became dependent upon potatoes to such a point that a fungi outbreak caused the starvation of approximately one million people from 1845 to 1849 in Ireland – known as the Potato Famine. The Irish were not only dependent upon potatoes; they were dependent on just a few varieties. This famine was a leading cause of migration to America. It serves as a reminder of the importance of biodiversity and sustainability.

Irish immigrants brought potatoes with them to America. In America, potatoes were slow to gain popularity. Americans feared potatoes and did not want what happened in Ireland to occur in America.

Botanist Louis Burbank saw the potential of the potato. He developed a new variety that grew better, was more productive, and more disease resistant. The Burbank underwent additional refinement to become the Russet potato. Today potatoes are a nationally grown vegetable valued for their durability, nutritional value, taste, and usability.

Competitive Advantage

Potatoes are popular. The average American eats 183 pounds of potatoes annually. It is a large crop virtually ignored by small-scale growers. *Nationwide potatoes are a 2.4 billion dollar business with very few brand standouts.* For heirloom growers, the diversity of the vegetable and the high consumer consumption make potatoes an opportunity.

Potatoes can be marketed directly to consumers, farm stands, or markets. Potatoes are waiting for an invitation to join the *farm-to-table* and *locally grown* movements. Consumers and restaurants often seek out "fresh" or "new" foods, and a new twist on this old favorite should boost sales of a premium-priced product.

Marketing and Sales Strategies

When marketing and selling potatoes, promote their health benefits. Potatoes are a great source of potassium. They are high in vitamin C and contain vitamin B6 along with more than 60 phytochemicals and vitamins.

Potatoes are an excellent choice for cross-selling and merchandising strategies. For example, potatoes go well with homemade butter and cheese and farm-fresh bacon, steaks, and poultry. Potatoes also do well as a value-added product such as potato salad or chips.

Potatoes offer year-round appeal. In the spring, red or fresh potatoes add great color to Easter meals. In the summer, grilled potatoes or potato salad are great for picnics. In the fall, potatoes quickly transform into hearty soups. Thanksgiving and Christmas dinners are not complete without mashed potatoes and gravy or potato casseroles. Baked potatoes are great year-round and go with just about anything or stand alone as an easy meal.

Production and growing

- **Soil and pH** - Potatoes grow best in deep soil that is loose and well-drained. The optimal potato pH is 5.5 to 6.5.
- **Nutrients** – Nitrogen (N) management is one of the most critical inputs for high-yielding, high-quality potato production. Potassium (P) is vital for tubular production. Phosphorus (P) improves potato flavor. Potatoes require fertilizer when planted and then again as tubulars develop.
- **Water** - Potatoes are mostly water, requiring 1 to 2 inches of water per week. The soil should remain moist but not wet. Potatoes do best with shallow and regular irrigation.

- **Spacing** - Tubers need room to grow. Seed potatoes need to be 3-inches deep and 12-inches apart within the rows, leaving about 3 feet of space between them. The only exception is when using straw bales or other growing mediums.
- **Growing Temp** - Potatoes grow best when temperatures are 45 to 80 degrees. Hot weather decreases the number of tubulars. If growing in hot climates, plant early enough for the tubulars to beat the heat. Planting potatoes 4 to 6 weeks before the last frost gives growers a head start. A second or third planting should happen after the last frost to ensure an extended season.
- **Pests** – The most common potato pests are potato beetles, flea beetles, aphids, leafhoppers, wireworms, and corn borers.
- **Disease** – Potato diseases include early blight, late blight, common and powdery scab, blackleg, leaf roll, mosaic viruses, Rhizoctonia, verticillium wilt, fusarium dry rot, and bacterial soft rot.
- **Hardiness Zones** - Potatoes do well in zones 1-7.
- **Tips** - Potatoes require full sun—plant in rows that allow for proper drainage. If you are cutting up potato pieces for planting, do so 1 to 2 days ahead of planting. It will give them the chance to "heal" and form a protective layer over the cut surface, improving moisture retention and rot resistance.
- **Harvest** –Actual harvest depends on the variety and use. Harvest potatoes from mid-July through October in the northeastern United States. A potato plant yields six

regular-size potatoes along with many smaller potatoes. Use a spaded fork when flowers are fading or when leaves turn yellow, or after the foliage has died. Transport potatoes tenderly to avoid bruising or damaging the skins.

Companion Plants

Potatoes do well with sage, coriander, catnip, green beans, cabbage, and corn. Sage will keep flea beetles away. Coriander, catnip, and green beans are good choices for warding off the Colorado potato beetle. Also, green beans add nitrogen to the soil, boosting potato growth.

The following plants improve potato taste: cabbage, corn, beans, and horseradish. In addition to added flavor, horseradish protects potatoes from diseases. Other vegetables that do well with potatoes are scallions, lettuce, and spinach.

Potatoes need to avoid raspberries, tomatoes, cucumbers, squash, and pumpkins. These plants tend to make potatoes more susceptible to blight. When rotating crops, avoid areas that have recently (within two years) had nightshade plants. Other problem plants are carrots, asparagus, fennel, turnip, onions, and sunflowers.

Uses

Potatoes are food. Potatoes and milk provide all the nutrients needed to sustain life. By frying, grilling, broiling, boiling, smoking, roasting, or baking them, one can never grow tired of them. As an ingredient, potatoes are appetizers, side dishes, and main dishes. As for comfort food, potatoes are great in casseroles, mashed, or salads.

Potatoes make great value-added items. Locally grown potato chips offer great marketing options. Potato salad and summer cookouts always go together. Potato soups make an excellent item for canning. People's love of premade potato items creates the potential for a standalone business.

Potatoes have medical uses. For example, raw potato juice helps with stomach ailments. Potatoes produce an enzyme that controls appetite. Raw potatoes treat issues such as arthritis, infections, burns, and sore eyes.

Fun Facts

- Nicknames for potatoes include tater and spud.
- Wild potatoes are poisonous.
- The Potato Museum is in Blackfoot, Idaho.
- During the 1600s, a common belief was witches were responsible for edible potatoes because they are part of the nightshade family.
- Potatoes are 80% water.
- The largest harvest from a single potato plant was 370 pounds.

- The single largest potato was 7 pounds 1 ounce.
- Old-timers in New England planted potato crops when dandelions bloomed.
- A wise tale states that planting potatoes on Good Friday wards off evil spirits.
- The time to cook a potato was a time unit for the Incas.
- The Prussians named the Bavarian Succession of 1778-79 the potato war.
- The potato was the first vegetable grown in space.
- Humans can survive on milk and potatoes.
- Potatoes have more Vitamin C than an orange, more potassium than a banana, and more fiber than an apple.
- The world's largest potato chip was 23 inches x 14.5 inches.
- Potatoes grow in all 50 states.
- The word potato comes from the Spanish word patata.
- China is the leading producer of potatoes.
- Potatoes starred in the movie Martian.
- Mr. and Mrs. Potato Head are popular toys.

Selected Varieties

Adirondack Blue Deep Potato is a mid-season heirloom with deep purple skin and flesh whose tuber is round, oblong, or slightly flattened. The meat is moist and delicious, and perfect for mashing. It sustains its striking color when cooked. Its storability makes it a fine choice for market growers.

Bamberger Hörnchen is a mid-season heirloom from Bamberg, Germany. It is a crucial ingredient in many German-Jewish dishes. This potato almost went extinct and is very hard to find outside of its home in Bamberg; it's a finger-shaped potato from the late 1880s. This potato has a nutty, aromatic flavor.

Bintje Potato is a mid-season heirloom from the Netherlands, where it was developed in the early 1900s. It produces oblong tubers with thin skin and shallow eyes. This very productive plant consistently produces very high yields. It is a very chic western European heirloom that should do great in most American markets.

Early Ohio Potato is an early season heirloom from the late 1800s; it is perfect for Ohio's cooler climate. This medium-sized potato produces round tubers with a light color. It is a popular heirloom for many backyard gardeners and is poised to become a local food favorite. This multipurpose potato does well baked, boiled, or fried. It has excellent storability and stores well for 3 - 4 months.

Early Rose Potato is an early-season heirloom from the early 1880s. Bred by Vermont farmer Albert Bresee in 1861, this potato is the foundation of many commercial potatoes. The Early Rose has smooth tubers with red skin and white flesh. It is not an excellent choice for the Deep South or west because excessive heat limits tuber production, quantity, and size.

German Butterball is a late-season German heirloom. It is a multipurpose potato whose flesh is flaxen. The buttery flavor makes it a delicious choice for mashing or baking. It is one of the best-tasting heirloom varieties.

Green Mountain Potato is a late-season heirloom with brunet skin with white flesh. This potato dates back to the 1880s and is the perfect potato for New England cuisine. The green mountain potato is the ideal choice for gratin potatoes, Rösti, pones, or potato chips. This potato stores exceptionally well.

Irish Cobbler Potato is an early season heirloom with tan skin and an irregular form. It is a classic Irish potato that is the central component of many Irish dishes. Its bright white skin combined with deep-seated eyes makes it excellent for mashing or baking. It has a subtle nutty flavor allowing for an enriching meal.

Katahdin is a late-season heirloom from Maine that has a russet skin. It is known for its resistance to viruses and its ability to diverse environments. It is a delectable potato that is a very trustworthy producer. The waxy flesh of the Katahdin is superb boiled or used in potato salad.

Kennebec Potato is a late-season heirloom with tan skin that is resilient to viruses and blight. This potato has been trending as a fry tossed in truffle oil. It is a trendy item in food circles. This potato is very high yielding making economic sense to grow.

Magic Molly Purple is an early to late-season heirloom. When young, this works well as a fingerling. When mature, this works well as a baking potato. The Magic Molly keeps its purple color when boiled. This potato has a nice earthy flavor.

Mountain Rose is an early-season heirloom with red skin and pink flesh. This potato is virus-resistant and easy to grow. The Mountain Rose has pink flesh because of the higher than average level of antioxidants. The Mountain Rose is well-liked among chefs and food lovers and makes a novel farm-to-table item.

Norland Potato is an early red skin heirloom that is scab resilient. This potato works wonders for boiling, adding to roast, or making potato salad. Famous for its great storability and it sells well at most markets. This potato is consistent in size, shape, and color.

Peach Blow Potato is a late-season heirloom requiring 120 frost-free days. This heirloom survived the potato famine making it one of the oldest heirlooms available. The name comes from its peach-colored flowers. Peach-blow produces small potatoes with excellent flavor.

Red Pontiac Potato is a mid-season red heirloom from Michigan. This potato boils well and serves best either whole or mashed. This familiar-looking potato moves well in most markets.

Rose Finn Apple is an early season heirloom from the Andes Mountains. Foodies, chefs, and gourmet markets seek out this highly admired heirloom. The tubers are medium-sized, long and narrow, easy to slice, and easy to roast. This variety requires a little more fertilizer and water for results, but it is worth the extra work. This potato has above-average storability.

Russet Burbank Potato is a late-season heirloom from the mid-1800s. Developed as a response to the Great Potato Famine of Ireland, this classic potato is excellent for baking or frying, especially French fries. These potatoes require cool nights and loose soil to thrive – a classic that has stood the test of time.

Shetland Black Potato is a dark purple heirloom from the Shetland Islands developed during the Victorian era. It is a popular UK potato but rare in the States. It is tasty and fluffy while adding a creative flair to potato-based dishes.

Strawberry Paw Potato is a mid-season heirloom that does best when boiled and used in potato salad. It is an attractive potato with red skin and creamy white flesh. Considered one of the best tasting varieties around, it is a clever choice for a potato display.

Viking Potato is a mid-season heirloom with deep red to purple skin. This potato produces high yields of gorgeous potatoes. The tubers of this plant are quite large. This potato does not perform well in clay soils. It must have loose sandy loam soil with lots of organic material; it also does well in containers or raised beds. One year, I grew this, and at my farmstand, I had one of these guys dressed up as Viking. It was a fun conversation starter.

Pumpkin

"For plainly 'tis seen the Pumpkin is Queen of the ranch and the dinner table..." ~**May C. Hanks**

Pumpkins are fall royalty. Pumpkin celebration starts in September when pumpkin spice lattes appear in coffee shops, followed by Jack-O-Lanterns in October and Pumpkin pie for Thanksgiving and Christmas. The pumpkins' role is to usher in autumn and mark the beginning of the end of another growing year while celebrating harvest time.

Pumpkin season is a time of reflection. Pumpkin season is a time of planning. As pumpkins harvest, it is time to think about the previous year. What worked well, what did not work well, what was lost, and gained. Pumpkin harvest means it is time to plan for next year.

History

Pumpkins have been a North American staple for 10,000 years. The earliest North American natives used wild pumpkins to store food and water. In the beginning, only the pumpkin seeds were edible; however, through thousands of years of selective breeding, its flesh became edible.

Pumpkins spread to Europe during the age of exploration. Pumpkins were first widely used in France as a pie filling. From France, pumpkins made their way through the rest of Europe. When pumpkins arrived in Ireland, they replaced turnips and potatoes for use as Jack-O-Lanterns. Today pumpkins flavor drinks, make pies, bread, and decorations. They have achieved icon status.

Competitive Advantage

Pumpkins have been increasing in popularity over the past few years. According to industry research, pumpkin sales increased by 10% from 2016 to 2017.

Pumpkins are a great way to extend a farm's cash flow well into the fall. Depending on the variety and size of pumpkin grown, growers can expect up to 1,600 pumpkins per acre. The larger the pumpkin, the fewer the pumpkins a grower will have per acre and vice versa.

Ways of making profits with pumpkins include selling at roadside stands, farmers markets, and wholesale. To maximize revenue, create an experience. Pumpkin patches emotionally engage with customers. You are not just selling pumpkins; you are providing memories for your customers.

People look forward to taking kids to pumpkin patches. This wholesome fall time activity creates memories. This agritourism approach allows growers to earn retail prices for pumpkins. Also, there are add-on items such as tractor and hayrides, petting zoos, value-added products, farm tours, corn mazes, games, and so on.

Pumpkin patches are great not only for families but for groups. Pumpkin patches are field trip opportunities for schools, churches, and home school organizations, among others. Pumpkin patches can be teambuilding or culture-building activities for employers or as an employee benefit.

For growers and produce sellers, pumpkin patches are a way to build customer loyalty. *Today's customers are looking for more than a tangible product; they are looking for an experience.* Pumpkin patches are a great way to give customers an adventure and to turn them into friends.

Marketing and Sales Strategies

Pumpkins sell according to size, weight, and use. The tiniest pumpkins are miniature pumpkins that grow up to 4 inches in diameter and weigh less than a pound. Small pumpkins weigh 1 to 5 pounds. Medium pumpkins weigh 5 to 10 pounds. Large pumpkins weigh 10 - 25 pounds, and mammoth or giant pumpkins weigh over 25 pounds and reach 100 pounds.

Typically, miniature pumpkins make incredible fall decorations. People like small pumpkins for decorations or Jack-O-Lanterns. Cook small pumpkins with the tops cut off with milk, sugar, and cinnamon as a treat. Use medium to large pumpkins for decorations, cooking, preserving, or as Jack-O-Lanterns.

To increase pumpkin sales, offer recipes and ideas for pumpkin-themed goods such as pies, breads, and cakes. During Halloween, pumpkin promotion needs to focus on large pumpkins for jack-o-lanterns and small pumpkins for decorating.

Contact local schools and groups and offer samples as a way to attract people to your pumpkin patch. Offer teachers a deal on a class size group of small pumpkins – many lower elementary teachers buy the tiny pumpkins for their students' Halloween class parties. You will create a lot of goodwill if you make them a good deal. Halloween promotions should be festive and fun. From Halloween to Christmas, focus on value-added products that people can give as gifts, such as pumpkin pies and breads.

While many people think of pumpkins as a festive fall item, a way to extend the pumpkin season before and after October is to market the pumpkins' health benefits. Pumpkins are high in beta-carotene, a good source of fiber, and contain vitamin A.

Production and growing

- **Soil and pH** - Pumpkins grow well in sandy loam soil that is slightly acidic with lots of organic material. The optimal pumpkin pH is 5.5 to 7.0.
- **Nutrients** - Pumpkin needs nitrogen (N). For best results, use a 5-10-5 fertilizer at planting and reapply monthly.
- **Water** - Pumpkins are mostly water and require a steady supply of water. Pumpkin roots tend to be deep, and the

soil should be moist 4 inches below the surface. Drip irrigation is best for pumpkins. It gives the water time to soak into the ground. A general rule of thumb for pumpkins is 1 to 1 ½ inches per week and more during dry conditions.

- **Spacing** - Whether in rows or beds, pumpkins need to be 5-feet apart in all directions.
- **Growing Temp** - Pumpkins do not tolerate frost at all and grow well in hot weather. Pumpkin seeds germinate when temperatures are between 60 - 105 degrees. Seeds will not germinate in cool soil. To maximize the growing season, start indoors.
- **Pests** - Squash bugs are the biggest problem for pumpkins. Other pests include the spotted, striped, and banded cucumber beetles. The squash vine borer is a dangerous pest that can quickly kill pumpkin plants.
- **Disease** - Bacterial wilt is problematic for pumpkin plants; this starts with wilting leaves followed by the plant quickly dying. Powdery mildew is another challenging disease. Blossom-end rot appears as a dark-colored dry rot on the end of the fruit where the flower attaches.
- **Hardiness Zones** - Pumpkins grow in all USDA hardiness zones.
- **Tips** - Plant pumpkins for Halloween from late May in northern locations to early July in southern sites. Pumpkin seeds should be planted with 4 to 5 seeds per hill and then thinned to 2 or 3 plants per hill. Pumpkins

require full sun and good drainage, feed on compost, and need weeding – the best weed control is light mulch.

- **Harvest** – Harvest when pumpkins reach the desired color and size. Use a knife to cut the pumpkin stem from the vine leaving enough stem for a handle.

Companion Plants

Corn is a good companion plant for pumpkins; plant in advance to ensure it grows taller than the pumpkin plants. Beans are good to plant with pumpkins as pumpkins benefit from nitrogen. Herbs such as peppermint, dill, oregano, etc., protect it from harmful pests and is a solid practice for urban growers concerned with space.

Pumpkins have broad leaves that block the sun, therefore, avoid low-growing crops. Pumpkins are greedy. They will steal moisture and nutrients from other plants. Potatoes and pumpkins should never be close to each other. They are antagonistic with each other, and both will suffer as they aggressively steal resources.

Uses

Pumpkins have many cooking uses. Virtually all parts of the plant are edible. The most popular pumpkin use is pie, but the flowers, leaves, and rinds are useable. Native Americans boiled, roasted, mashed, and made soup out of all parts of the pumpkin. Cooking green or immature pumpkins in the same savory fashion as summer squash is a delicacy.

Pumpkins have many medicinal uses. The sap and pulp of pumpkins treat burns. Pumpkin seeds are diuretic. Native Americans used pumpkins to treat intestinal worms and urinary infections. Traditional Chinese medicine use pumpkins to treat parasites, including tapeworms.

Pumpkins have many decorative uses. Use tiny pumpkins to accent Halloween and Thanksgiving themes. Use small pumpkins for bookends, paint them, or cover them with glitter. Use medium to large pumpkins with cornstalks to create an entryway display. Carve pumpkins into Jack-O-Lanterns. Use the process of decorating pumpkins as a great family or child-centered activity.

Fun Facts

- Pumpkins are a good source of potassium and Vitamin A.
- Native Americans dried pumpkin strips and used the dried rinds to make mats and clothing.
- The largest pumpkin pie weighed 350 pounds.

- Pumpkin used to be a piecrust ingredient.
- Pumpkin flesh adds moisture and is an oil substitute.
- People thought pumpkins could remove freckles.
- People thought pumpkins could treat snakebites.
- The largest recorded pumpkin weighed 1,140 pounds.
- Eighty percent of US pumpkin sales are in October.
- Roasted pumpkin seeds are a great snack.
- Pumpkins make nutritious animal feed.
- Pumpkins range in size from less than a pound to over 1,000 pounds.
- In colonial times, Native Americans roasted long strips of pumpkin in an open fire.
- Illinois produces over four hundred million pounds of pumpkins annually.
- The top three pumpkin states are Illinois, Ohio, Pennsylvania, and California.

Selected Varieties

Americana Tonda Squash is an ornamental heirloom with orange skin and green stripes between the ribs. This small pumpkin weighs up to 6 pounds. The Padana Squash has orange flesh, is sweet, dry, and great for soup or roasting.

Amish Pie Pumpkin is a baking pumpkin from the Amish community in Maryland. It is a hefty fruit with sweet flesh that weighs up to 80 pounds. The Amish claim just one pumpkin can feed an Amish community! The Amish Pie Pumpkin is excellent for making puree and canning, freezing, or other culinary uses. It is a good seller with a great marketing story.

Atlantic Giant Pumpkin is a novelty heirloom used to set records. The largest Atlantic Pumpkin was just over 2,600 pounds. It is a good pumpkin for pumpkin patch growers who can use these pumpkins as attention getters. The primary use of this pumpkin is as a spectacle.

Big Max Pumpkin is a multipurpose heirloom that grows large and amazes customers because of its massiveness. It is an excellent choice for carving or baking. This pumpkin can easily reach 100 pounds. It is perfect for pumpkin patch growers who want to impress customers. These pumpkins make stunning displays.

Black Futsu Pumpkin is a rare ornamental heirloom from Japan. This Japanese pumpkin has deeper than typical ridges with warts and a deep, black-green rind that turns orange with age. This spooky-looking 3 to 5-pound pumpkin is perfect for Halloween. This pumpkin is a butternut squash substitute.

Casper Pumpkin is a ghostly white heirloom. This friendly pumpkin is easy to carve and paint, making it an excellent choice for decorations. This outstandingly sweet pumpkin makes a great pie or bread. This pumpkin has marketing potential.

Cheronskaya Pumpkin is an heirloom from Ukraine. This ghostly gray pumpkin makes for a scary Jack-O-Lantern. This pumpkin is easy to carve or paint. The seeds of this pumpkin make a great treat with just a little salt and olive oil. The flesh is sweet and makes an impressive pie filling. This matchless gray pumpkin will make any product mix more appealing and exciting.

Cinderella Pumpkin is a classic heirloom pumpkin. In the Cinderella story, this pumpkin is a smooth-skinned pumpkin with solid orange skin and flesh. It is attractive enough on its own to be a decoration but easy to crave. Its great tasting seeds and meat makes a tremendous value-added pie, bread, or cookie.

Connecticut Field Pumpkin is an heirloom from the 1700s. It is one of the oldest and most productive heirlooms. It is the most patriotic pumpkin, and if the pilgrims had their way, instead of saying as American as apple pie, we would be saying as American as pumpkin pie.

Fairytale Pumpkin is an 1800 French heirloom that is the inspiration of many fairy tales. The Fairytale Pumpkin offers haunting lobes renowned for their color, hue, and taste. This French heirloom grows up to 15 pounds, an excellent choice for decorating and cooking.

Flat White Boer Pumpkin is a South Africa heirloom. This pumpkin gets its name from the Dutch Boers, who were in power during colonial times. This adorable pumpkin is flat, white, and tasty. And a great decorating and carving item. This colossal pumpkin grows up to 30 pounds. Adding this pumpkin to your lineup will give more dimension, depth, and diversity to any display.

Galeux D'Eysines Pumpkin is a French heirloom from the 1700s. It is popular as winter squash and makes regular appearances in French soups. This pumpkin tastes much like a sweet potato with a slightly nutty flavor. This warty fruit with salmon-colored flesh makes for a charming pumpkin that attracts customers; it can grow up to 15 pounds.

Jack-O-Lantern Pumpkin is an American heirloom. For at least a century, this is the go-to pumpkin for carving. It makes delicious pies, muffins, and bread. It is the number one pumpkin grown in Illinois. Jack-O-Lantern is a good producer, and local growers can take advantage of this popularity by cutting out the intermediary and shipping costs.

Jarrahdale Pumpkin is a New Zealand heirloom. This pumpkin is a light blue to blue-gray color with a yellow to orange flesh. This pumpkin's deep ribs give the smooth skin a classic pumpkin shape. This good decorating pumpkin has an exceptionally long shelf life. This fruit grows up to 10 pounds and is productive producing 3 - 5 pumpkins per vine.

Kamo Kamo Pumpkin is a New Zealand heirloom. This pumpkin goes by the alias Kumi Kumi pumpkin. New Zealanders typically grill, fry, or bake the immature fruits. As the fruit matures, it develops all the classic pumpkin traits with a yellow/orange rind with dots and green splashes.

The flesh of this pumpkin has a nutty flavor. This pumpkin is becoming rare even in its home country of New Zealand. It is an excellent choice for growers interested in biodiversity and saving unique varieties of plant life.

Kentucky Field Pumpkin is an heirloom from the bluegrass state. It is a non-uniform pumpkin whose variations in sizes and shapes adds visual appeal to pumpkin patches and roadside stands. These fruits can grow up to 15 pounds and look like large bowling pins or candy corns. Growers like this pumpkin because it is productive, has a great shelf life, is a good shipper, and tastes great.

Marina Di Chioggia Pumpkin is an heirloom from the Northeast coast of Italy. It is rare outside of Italy and a good choice for growers looking for a unique item. This dual-purpose pumpkin has a classic bumpy exterior. This pumpkin looks like it is out of a Brothers Grimm story. Italians bake this pumpkin, a productive pumpkin that increases sales.

Musquee de Provence Pumpkin is a French heirloom. Vaughan's Seed Store in Chicago introduced this cheese pumpkin, because of its shape, to America in 1899. It is an interesting-looking pumpkin with deep orange flesh and is excellent for cooking. This pumpkin grows up to 20 pounds with deep ridges.

Nantucket Pie Pumpkin is a Maine heirloom that grows up to 8 pounds. It stores well and makes mouthwatering pie. Unlike other pumpkins, the Nantucket ripens off the vine allowing farther transportation than other pumpkins.

Omaha Pumpkin is an heirloom from the Omaha tribe. This pumpkin produces oblong 3-pound fruit. The Omaha pumpkin is easy to decorate and is a good carving pumpkin that makes a great Jack-O-Lantern.

This pumpkin is remarkable in pies and other baked items. It is an excellent pumpkin to bake whole with milk, sugar, and spices. Overall, this is a fabulous pumpkin with a great marketing story.

Sweet Kikuza Pumpkin is a Japanese heirloom with a slightly spicy kick. This hint of spicy-sweet makes this pumpkin a delectable choice for baking or roasting. Grown in America since the early 1900s, this pumpkin is good for markets with Japanese or Western Asia influences.

Thai Rai Kaw Tok Pumpkin is a green heirloom from Thailand. This pumpkin produces green fruits with tan spots. The flesh of this pumpkin is yellow/orange with a sweet taste and with a smooth texture. It is a fine-looking pumpkin for eating and is an excellent southern grower. It is easy to grow and withstands pests and disease. Also, it has good storability with a tough rind.

Winter Luxury Pie Pumpkin is an heirloom introduced by Johnson & Stokes in 1893. This pumpkin is a golden-colored 6-pounder – glorious for pie. It is an excellent choice for farm-to-table growers looking for a great value-added product or a great story to go with a delicious product.

Seminole Pumpkin is an heirloom from the Florida Everglades. When immature, this pumpkin is fried, grilled, roasted, or baked. When mature, it is like any other pumpkin. The Seminole pumpkin has light ribs with a light tan, almost cream exterior. The fruits of this plant grow up to 5 pounds, and it consistently has enormous yields.

Spinach

"Popeye was right about spinach: dark green, leafy vegetables are the healthiest food on the planet. As whole foods go, they offer the most nutrition per calorie." ~ Michael Greger

Spinach is inconspicuously wonderful. Spinach has a great leadership lesson: the best leaders do not seek the spotlight. The best leaders maintain a level of humility and give credit to other people. The best leaders support their people.

Spinach is nurturing. Leaders need to nurture their followers. Leadership is about bringing out the best in people while building your business. Growing spinach and growing your farm require planning, weeding, watering, fertilizing, and harvesting.

Spinach is working its way onto many salad bars. It is versatile and easily adaptable for healthy vegetable drinks, smoothies, or cooked as a side dish, added to soups or appetizers.

Spinach is a cool-weather, fast-growing plant related to beets. It is highly productive and grows in the spring or fall and during the Deep South's winter.

History

Spinach originated in the Middle East. The Persians were the first recorded users of spinach, and their word for it was aspanakh. From Persia, spinach made its way to 7th century China. The Moors brought spinach to Spain in 711, and over the next 700 years, spinach became Spanish. During this time, spinach spread to the rest of Europe.

During the 16th century, spinach became the favorite vegetable of Catherine de Medici of the famous Medici family of the Italian Renaissance. When she left her home in Florence to marry King Henry II of France, she brought her cooks, who brought spinach, which established the phrase "à la Florentine."

North Americans began growing spinach in the early 19th century. In the 20th century, the cartoon character, Popeye, who gained incredible strength whenever he ate a can of spinach, popularized spinach. Spinach is now a super popular superfood. It is trendy with people that are health conscious (for a good reason!).

Competitive Advantage

According to the USDA, spinach sales are increasing at a rate of 1.5%. In 2017, spinach averaged $4.55 a pound. Forty percent of grocery store customers reported purchasing spinach in the past year. Of those that purchased spinach, 45% stated a preference for baby spinach.

People visiting framer's markets are more interested in spinach than the typical grocery store customer is. Spinach purchasing increases as household income, with people in the highest income range being twice as likely to buy spinach.

People with higher incomes tend to be less price-sensitive and are more likely to exchange prices for quality. For a small grower, this means more profit for the same amount of effort.

Spinach is more gourmet and sophisticated than lettuce. People who seek out spinach tend to be health-conscious, trendy, or early adopters. Spinach consumers want to be actively engaged in the farm-to-table movement and want to connect with a farmer.

Spinach appeals to sophisticated customers because it is nutrient-dense, versatile, and flavorful. Raw spinach finds its way into salads, on top of sandwiches or tacos, and cooked spinach finds its way onto pizzas, quiches, or casseroles. Sautéed or steamed spinach is a side dish, and creamed spinach finds its way into spinach and artichoke dip.

Spinach is a fighter. If fights cancer. It is high in folate and can protect the brain from aging. Spinach promotes heart health and lowers cholesterol. Spinach even keeps skin and eyes healthy.

Marketing and Sales Strategies

Marketing spinach in the spring starts with holidays such as Passover, Easter, and Mother's Day. In the spring, spinach is great for omelets, quiches, dips, side dishes, or salads. Spring spinach is just beginning, as spinach is freshest in the spring. Springtime is the perfect time to sell baby spinach.

Summer spinach needs to feature its use as a sandwich topping or for summer salads (while it lasts). Summer's heat will slow down or even eliminate spinach production. Remind customers that Mother Nature gives spinach the summer off, and they should purchase spinach while they can.

Fall spinach needs to be marketed as a healthy school lunch, snack, or dip for tailgating parties. Spinach is a great weight loss item, with many people seeking it out for this purpose. During the fall, spinach is on the rebound. It is a great time to introduce value-added spinach products.

Offer winter spinach as something to use in soups or as a hearty side dish. A greenhouse can keep spinach producing deep into the winter.

It is a great idea to offer multiple spinach types, and one of those offerings must be baby spinach. Clamshell containers or pre-bagged spinach are great options for most markets for two reasons. First, it makes for a more visually appealing display. Secondly, it reduces transaction times, making it easier to serve more customers.

When packaging spinach, it is vital to leave some air space around the bags. Place spinach near other salad vegetables. Consider placing it next to red or yellow bell peppers or tomatoes to create an eye-catching color contrast.

Educate consumers about the many health benefits of spinach by displaying signs touting them. Create recipe cards so people can experiment with spinach. Samples are always a great strategy to move products. Offer a spinach dip with homemade bread to feature two products you sell at the same time.

Production and growing

- **Soil and pH** - Spinach grows best in well-drained soil rich in organic matter such as compost or composted manure. The optimal pH for spinach is 6.5 to 7.0.
- **Nutrients** - Spinach requires nitrogen (N), calcium (Ca), and iron (Fe). Nitrogen encourages growth, calcium promotes cell development, and iron develops deep green leaves. A general rule of thumb for spinach is 2 pounds of fertilizer per 100 square feet.
- **Water** - Spinach requires a steady supply of water. It needs water a few times a week for a total of 1 inch per week.
- **Spacing** – Place spinach 12 inches apart in rows that are 2 to 3 feet apart. If growing in beds, spinach needs to be 12 inches apart in all directions.
- **Growing Temp** - Spinach grows best when temperatures range between 60°F and 65°F. Spinach can withstand frost

and temperatures as low as 20 degrees. Spinach will bolt when temperatures rise above 80 degrees.

- **Pests** - Aphids love spinach. Baby click beetles or wireworms will munch on the leaves. Crown mites are problematic because they are nearly invisible because of their size.
- **Disease** - Common spinach diseases are white rust, blue mold (downy mildew), and fusarium wilt.
- **Hardiness Zones** - Spinach grows in all hardiness zones as an annual.
- **Tips** - Rotating spinach with unrelated crops for at least three years is the best control for fusarium wilt. Sow spinach every 10 to 14 days for a steady harvest of tender young leaves. Spinach, especially the crinkled leaf varieties, hangs onto the soil. Wash well before using.
- **Harvest** – Spinach is harvestable six to eight weeks after planting from plants with six or more 3 to 4-inch leaves. To harvest, carefully cut the outside leaves to prolong the plants' productivity, particularly with fall crops. Harvest the entire plant when it begins bolting. Once bolted, spinach becomes bitter.

Companion Plants

Spinach and beans do great together. Beans affix nitrogen to the soil while providing shade. It also does well with broccoli, Brussel sprouts, cabbage, and cauliflower.

Spinach likes eggplant, leeks, lettuce, melons, peas, potatoes, radishes, tomatoes, nasturtium, and strawberries. These plants offer shade or shelter for spinach while conserving moisture, controlling weeds, and providing disease or insect protection. These plants have different nutritional needs, so there is less competition for food.

Few if any plants are a problem to plant with spinach.

Uses

Spinach is a primary food source for pasta, soups, and casseroles. Spinach gives many foods the illusion of healthy eating. It is why it appears in foods such as wraps, breads, and chips.

Spinach has many health benefits, controls glucose levels, and reduces cancer risk while improving bone health. Spinach contains an antioxidant known as alpha-lipoic acid, which helps manage diabetes.

Fun Facts

- Americans consume nearly 2.5 pounds of spinach per year.
- Spinach has 0g of fat.
- Spinach also has flavonoids, phytonutrients that slow down the division of cancer cells in the human stomach and cancer cells of the skin.

- Spinach makes people smarter by increasing blood flow to the brain.
- Spinach is a wound healer.
- Spinach increases metabolism.
- The spinach capital of the world is Crystal City, Texas.
- Spinach became popular with the endorsement of Popeye.
- In Medieval days, painters used spinach to make green paint.
- The first commercially available vegetable was spinach.
- A half-cup of cooked spinach contains 10% of your daily-recommended value of iron.
- There are three basic types of spinach: savoy (curly leaves), semi-savoy (not so curly leaves), and flat (smooth flat leaves).

Selected Varieties

Amsterdam Prickly Spinach is a flat-leaved European heirloom. This spinach was introduced in America when Jefferson featured it at Monticello. This spinach was very popular in the 19th century because it was slow to bolt and tolerated light frost.

Modernized food transportation and the need for standardization pushed this spinach out of favor. Bunching spinach became popular because it was easier to store and transport. This spinach is an excellent choice for the locally grown movement. This spinach produces intriguing triangle leaves with red-tinged stalks.

Beet Perpetual Spinach. It is a beet used and marketed like spinach. The leaves of this heirloom have a traditional spinach flavor. When small, it is baby spinach. This beet can grow for two years providing many leaves for food. It is a good variety because of its high productivity.

Bloomsdale Long Spinach is a savoy heirloom that has been a standard since its introduction in the 1920s. This spinach is slow to bolt, travels well, and merchandises great when bunched. The leaves of this plant are glossy dark green and mouthwatering. This spinach is very popular among chefs and food lovers.

Butterflay Spinach is a savoy heirloom from Germany. This spinach is slow to bolt and is a great choice for spring or overwinter planting. It has a deep green color, and it is one of the more flavorful heirlooms. This spinach is good whether used raw in a salad, cooked, or frozen.

Galilee Spinach is a flat heirloom from Israel that is heat tolerant and slow to bolt, perfect for the south. It produces dark green triangle-shaped leaves. When young, it is a delicious baby spinach. The mature version of this spinach needs cooking. This spinach is a popular choice in markets with people who are interested in Mediterranean diets.

Gigante d'Inverno Spinach or Giant of Winter is a savoy heirloom from Italy. It is perfect spinach for pasta, dips, and other Italian dishes. This frost-tolerant heirloom produces well into the winter. This plant consistently has large, broad, deep green leaves that look great when bunched.

Merlo Nero Spinach is a savoy heirloom from Italy whose name means blackbird. This spinach grows only in cool weather and does not tolerate heat. It has a great classic Italian look, taste, and texture. The leaves of the Merlo Nero are dark green and rounded. This spinach is rare in the United States and could be a good option for winters in the south.

Monstrueux De Viroflay Spinach is a semi savoy heirloom with 10-inch long leaves. These leaves are mostly smooth with a dark green color. This fast-growing spinach is fall-planted and grows through the winter — a traditional French variety dating back to the 1860s.

New Zealand Spinach is not a spinach but a member of the fig-marigold family; however, it has been used as spinach since Fearing Burr introduced it in 1863. This leafy plant tolerates heat but not frost. For growers, this long-lasting product produces a spinach product after other varieties have bolted

Viking Spinach is a semi-savoy heirloom first introduced in 1933. This spinach has dark leaves and is a good choice for salads or steaming. This very productive plant produces many leaves. It is a cold-hardy plant that can tolerate some frost, but it will bolt during the hot summer months.

Viroflay Spinach a classic French Heirloom. It is large spinach that is delicious, easy growing, and adaptable. This spinach is rare in America, but it is one of the most popular varieties in France. This spinach has excellent marketing appeal and does well in the garden and kitchen.

Squash

*"You know, when you get your first asparagus, or your first acorn squash, or your first really good tomato of the season, those are the moments that define the cook's year. I get more excited by that than anything else." ~ **Mario Batali***

Squash is a lesson in diversity. Squash comes in many different shapes, sizes, colors, and types. Just like people come in many different shapes, sizes, colors, and styles.

Diversity brings out the best in systems. In nature, the most diverse ecosystems are the most productive and sustainable. In business, the most diverse businesses are the most productive and sustainable. In produce, the most diverse growers are the most productive and sustainable.

The two broadest types of squash are summer and winter. Summer squash grows on a bush and includes varieties such as zucchini, yellow squash, and zephyr. Summer squash is picked while it is immature, and the rind is edible. Winter squash is harvested when mature and the skin has hardened; examples include butternut, acorn, and spaghetti.

History

Squash is native to the new world. Squash entered human use as soon as people arrived in Central America. At first, it was for utility. Squash made great containers, dishes, and floats for fishing nets. Edible squash is the result of selective breeding. Squash provided the early people of North America a steady food source; when combined with maize and beans, it could sustain a village.

The Norte Chico people of ancient Peru first farmed squash. From Peru, squash spread to other parts of Mesoamerica. The Wampanoag Indians brought squash to the area now known as New England and essential to this tribe because it lasted all the winter. Other early adopters of North American squash were the Koster people in Illinois around 8,000 BC and the ancient people from Phillips Spring, Missouri, around 5,000 years ago. The Europeans introduced squash to Europe. From Europe, squash spread to the rest of the world.

Competitive Advantage

Fresh squash is a 150 million dollar a year market. Growing squash allows you to grow your business. Squash sales have increased since 2014, and current trends indicate squash sales will continue to grow.

High-end food is in vogue. These consumers are continually seeking out different varieties of all types of fresh produce. Rare squash buyers typically have higher incomes, and the vast number of available heirloom squash creates an opportunity to offer various products that appeal to high-end customers.

Squash is highly productive. Summer squash such as yellow squash or zucchini can produce 25 pounds of produce per plant. In 2018, the average price of squash at most farmers markets was $2.00 per pound. Therefore, a grower can make up to $50.00 a plant. Squash is so productive that it could be a loss leader to attract customers who will buy other items.

Marketing and Sales Strategies

Squash offers many marketing opportunities; for example, spaghetti squash is a replacement for high carb and highly processed noodles. During the summer, yellow squash and zucchini are excellent grilling options. During the fall and winter, squash is ideal for soup making.

To encourage customers to purchase squash, offer samples of different varieties and prepare informational and recipe cards of varying squash varieties. Even small efforts such as this engage your customers and create loyalty for your farm stand.

The adage is stack high, and watch it fly, and squash is very stackable. *Squash's multitudes of color make an attractive display.* Pre-packing squash with other items in value packs listed as spring vegetables, salad toppings, or stir-fry ingredients is a way to create a value-added product for customers.

Production and growing

- **Soil and pH** - Squash grows well in sandy loam soil that is slightly acidic with lots of organic material. The optimal squash pH is 5.5 to 7.0.
- **Nutrients** - Squash needs little nitrogen (N). Too much nitrogen causes deep green leaves with no blossoms. For best results, use a 5-10-5 fertilizer at planting and reapply monthly.
- **Water** - Squash is mostly water and requires a steady supply of water. Squash roots grow deep, and the soil should be moist 4 inches below the surface. A general rule of thumb for squash is 1 to 1 ½ inches per week and more during the summer, especially in dry conditions.
- **Spacing** - Whether in rows or beds, squash needs to be 3 feet apart in all directions.
- **Growing Temp** - Squash does not tolerate frost at all and does well in hot weather. Squash germinates when temperatures are 60 - 105 degrees. Seeds will not germinate in cool soil. To maximize the growing season, start indoors.

- **Pests** - Squash bugs are the biggest problem for squash. Squash bugs insert a toxin that kills the plant. Other pests include the spotted, striped, and banded cucumber beetles; they are very harmful to squash.
- **Disease** - Bacterial wilt, powdery mildew, and blossom-end rot are the most common squash diseases.
- **Hardiness Zones** - Squash grows in all USDA hardiness zones.
- **Tips** - Squash seeds should be planted with 4 to 5 seeds per hill and then thinned to 2 or 3 plants per hill. Squash requires full sun and good soil drainage. Squash likes to eat decomposing weeds and other plant material. A light mulch is the best pest control. When transplanting young seedlings in sunny weather, cover them with an upside-down pot or other shade covers for a few days to prevent wilting.
- **Harvest -** The type of squash determines harvested. Summer squash is best when young and tender before the seeds mature, and the rind hardens. Winter squash is best when the skin has toughened, and the seeds are mature.

Companion Plants

Corn is a good companion plant for squash. Beans are another good plant to put with squash as beans affix nitrogen to the soil. Also known as the three sisters planting combination introduced by Native Americans.

Herbs such as peppermint, dill, and oregano deter harmful pests. Planting close or in between squash provides the best results. For best results, plant tall companions before planting squash.

Summer squash has broad leaves that block out the sun. Low-growing crops such as lettuce, spinach, strawberries need a home elsewhere in the patch. Squash are heavy feeders that take moisture and nutrients from other plants.

Potatoes and squash should never be close to each other in the garden. Both plants are heavy feeders, and both plants attract the same pests. Other members of the squash family need their space so that cross-pollination does not occur.

Uses

Squash is a versatile vegetable. Squash has food, health, and practical uses. Squash improves vision, immune system, and bone strength. It also fights cancer, reduces inflammation, and lowers blood pressure.

Summer squash is great for cooking. Breads and cakes are value-added products that use summer squash. Squash is great for healthy French fries, grilled as a side dish, baked as the main course, or used raw in salads. Mature seeds baked with salt and olive oil are a healthy savory treat.

Winter squash is great for baking or soups. Casseroles are a value-added product that uses winter squash. Premade casseroles are convenient for customers while eliminating waste, and winter squash are great for decorations. People use winter squash as display accents, birdhouses, or crafts.

Squash and blossoms are edible and can be prepared in a variety of ways. Squash blossoms find their way into soups and stews, as well as being sautéed, stuffed, and dipped in batter and fried.

Fun Facts

- In 1768, French botanist A.N. Duchesne developed new squash varieties by hand cross-pollination.
- Squash is high in fiber and is an excellent food for weight loss.
- California is the largest squash producer in the United States.
- Winter squash is more nutritious than summer squash.
- Squash is mainly carbohydrates, little protein, and almost no fat.
- Botanical and folk medicine use squash seeds for various treatments.
- Joe Jutras grew a 2,118-pound green squash.
- The entire squash plant is edible.
- Presidents Washington and Jefferson both grew squash in their gardens.
- Squash candy is popular in Latin America.

- Just one cup of Squash has 42% of the daily vitamin C requirements.
- The United States is the world's leading importer of squash.

Selected Varieties

Acorn Squash is a winter squash that grows to be about five or six inches long and can weigh up to 2 pounds. This heirloom looks like a giant green acorn with orange bands. The orange meat is an attractive option for soups, baking, roasting, or as a casserole. This easy-to-grow squash is always an excellent choice to bring to market.

Banana Squash is a winter squash and a 4,000 year-old Central American heirloom. This giant elongated squash grows up to 3 feet long and weighs up to 40 pounds, and its skin is a pale yellow to light beige with bright orange flesh. In Central America, it is quartered and sold like watermelons. These large fruits are attention-getting at farmers markets.

Butternut Squash is a winter heirloom that is a seasonal favorite. A part of the Turban squash family (hard shells with turban-like shapes), this squash has a sweet orange flesh with green skin that turns beige as it ripens. Butternut squash has a stretched body with a bulb at the bottom. This popular winter heirloom is perfect for soups, risotto, baking, or ravioli.

Chirimen Squash is a winter heirloom from Japan's Edo period. A green squash that turns taupe when mature, Chirimen squash can grow up to 5 pounds with a flattened top and bottom. It is a great baking squash; rare even in its home country.

Cocozella Di Napoli Squash is an heirloom summer squash from Italy. It is a yellow striped zucchini and an excellent option for grilling, roasting, or baking. The flesh of this squash is green instead of white. It is a standard variety in Italy but rare in the United States.

Delicata Squash is a winter heirloom with summer squash potential. When immature, it is baked, roasted, or grilled. A green or orange striped fruit with cream-colored flesh, this squash grows up to 8 inches in length. This squash has a delicate rind, so it is tricky to transport. Delicata is also known as peanut, bohemian, or sweet potato squash. This squash weighs about one pound.

Hubbard Squash is a winter heirloom that is large and heavy with a wart-like appearance. This squash weighs up to 40 pounds. The flesh inside is a dense pale yellow with a delicate flavor. The exterior color is deep green, but it can come in white, blue-gray, and orange varieties. This squash is an attention-getter that will get people to stop at your stand.

Kabocha Squash is a winter heirloom from Japan with a sweet taste. It is a green-skin and yellow-orange meat member of the turban family that has a nutty flavor. It goes great in Japanese dishes. When taking to market, select solid and heavy for their size fruits; this squash is an excellent choice for roasting, soups, mashed, pies, and cakes.

Lakota Squash is a winter heirloom from the Lakota Sioux. It is a pear-shaped red squash with green streaks at the bottom. This great-tasting baking squash is suited for fall decorations whose flesh is fine-grained and sweet with a nutty taste. A great item to make fall farm stands attractive and inviting.

Orangetti Squash is a winter heirloom variation of spaghetti squash. This heirloom has an orange exterior and flesh. It is higher in Vitamin A than traditional yellow squash. It is a good choice for farm stands because it has the familiar characteristics of the well-known spaghetti squash while being different enough to stand out.

Pastila Shampan Squash is a winter heirloom from France. The name translates as "fruit-candy champagne." A sweet-tasting squash with a banana shape grows up to 18 inches and weighs up to 10 pounds. It is a good choice for pies, breads, or baking.

Pattypan Squash is a summer heirloom from France. This small squash grows only 2 inches in height. This squash comes in many different colors, varying from pale green to dark green, yellow, yellow with green, or white. It has grooved edges with creamy white flesh – a mild-tasting squash with many different culinary uses.

Spaghetti Squash is a winter variety with an elongated shape that grows up to 14 inches long. This popular squash is an excellent substitute for carb-rich pasta. This yellow fruit has a pale yellow flesh that becomes stringy when appropriately cooked. This squash stacks well, quickly creating a mountain of squash.

Scallop Squash is a popular winter squash that comes in many sizes, shapes, colors, and varieties. It has a round and shallow shape with scalloped edges and looks like a small toy top or flying saucer. Scallop squash is great fried or baked.

Sweet Dumpling Squash is a yellow to orange winter heirloom that is sweet and great for stuffing. It is a decorative item and creative container for serving soups, dips, and sauces. Some growers use these containers for farm stand displays.

Tatume Squash is a vine-growing summer heirloom. This squash is very popular in traditional Mexican cuisine. When picked tiny (about the size of a baseball), it is flavorful, like zucchini or yellow squash. Tatume is round to slightly elongated with green fruits. This plant is disease-resistant and productive.

Turban Squash is a dual-purpose winter heirloom. This decorative squash tastes as good as it looks. It is a Central American variety that is perfect for soup. This squash is available in orange, green, or white. The yellow-orange flesh has a sweet taste, and the hard shell of this squash doubles as a soup bowl. It is a great display item that makes an attractive fall decoration.

Yellow Straight or Crookneck is a classic summer heirloom. There are many different varieties with minor variations. This squash is best when 4 to 6 inches long. Yellow squash is a southern favorite for frying, relish, grilling, or roasting. When selling select firm, blemish-free fruits for best results.

Zucchini is a classic summer heirloom. Zucchini can be fried, grilled, roasted, or baked into breads, cakes, and cookies. Zucchinis are deep green and are best when picked 4 to 6 inches; however, some people prefer larger fruits for baking and stuffing. There are many different varieties of zucchinis with minor variations. Zucchini bread is a great value-added product.

Tomatoes

"You rarely get satisfaction sitting in an easy chair. If you work in a garden on the other hand, and it yields beautiful tomatoes, that's a good feeling." - **Dan Buettner**

Tomatoes give gardening purpose. People need a sense of purpose. Having a purpose is what gets people up out of bed. Having purpose drives the human experience. Having purpose moves people forward. Having purpose provides direction. Having purpose is everything.

Developing a perfect tomato is a purpose-driven activity. Heirloom tomatoes are the ideal tomatoes because they are better tasting, easier to grow, and better for the environment.

Heirloom tomatoes have personalities. Just as every person is unique, each heirloom tomato is unique. People and tomatoes should not be uniform objects from an assembly line. *There needs to be room for differences.* There needs to be room for innovations, and there needs to be room for excellence.

If you sell produce, you must sell tomatoes. People will get up early and drive miles for a good tomato. People will wait in line at dawn for homegrown tomatoes. Homegrown tomatoes have a very loyal following.

Tomatoes are either determinate (bush or limited height) or indeterminate (a vine that keeps growing). Tomatoes are annuals with some varieties ready in just 50 days.

Tomatoes grow well in warm weather conditions with lightweight, fertile soil, with plenty of organic matter added to the ground. They are the most productive when it is warm, and the soil temperature is consistently above 65 degrees.

History

The Aztecs first grew tomatoes in Peru around 700 A.D. From Peru, tomatoes made their way north to Mexico. By the age of discovery, tomatoes in central and South America. Spanish explorers brought tomatoes to Spain. From Spain, tomatoes spread slowly throughout Europe and the rest of the world.

Tomatoes did not become super popular until the 1880s when an Italian pizza maker put tomatoes on pizza. Tomatoes became sauce. This sauce mixed with cheese created the modern pizza. Tomato sauce, through the process of canning, became the basis for many other Italian dishes. From Italy, tomato-based foods spread to Europe and the rest of the world.

Competitive Advantage

People love tomatoes. At any farmers market, the vendors with homegrown vine-ripened tomatoes consistently outperform other vendors. Vendors that resell tomatoes do slightly better, and the vendors without tomatoes struggle for any sales. Homegrown heirloom tomatoes out-sell any other product at any farmers market.

Many growers routinely report that heirloom tomatoes will double and, in some cases, triple revenue. It is a good practice for growers to have more than one tomato variety. Some consumers follow tomato varieties and are very loyal to their favorite type. Heirloom tomatoes come in various sizes and shapes that can stack high and create a very eye-catching display.

It is imperative to be the first and last person at market with tomatoes. A hoop or greenhouse is vital to make this happen. A few additional weeks of tomatoes can add thousands of dollars of income. If growing in a hoop house or greenhouse, use soil and compost instead of hydroponics for a better-tasting product.

Marketing and Sales Strategies

The goal with tomato marketing and selling is to inform people that you have tomatoes, the types of tomatoes you grow, and the quantity you can supply.

Merchandising tomatoes is essential. Stacking tomatoes too high will bruise or damage ripe tomatoes. Many growers/marketers will use quart boxes to display tomatoes and sell by the quart instead of the pound.

Prepackaging tomatoes for busy markets allows growers to service more customers. More customers mean more transactions, and more transactions turn into more profit. Many growers have clamshell containers, brown bag tomatoes, box or other ready-to-go containers so a customer can quickly be on their way.

Tomatoes make a great pre-paid item. Many growers report selling out of tomatoes in just a few hours. To provide a higher level of service, growers can presell tomatoes and put the customer's name on a box or bag. It increases customer loyalty and frees up time to spend with new customers. This technique can double produce sales. The key is to have one person that just deals with the pre-orders and another person or two dealing with walk-up customers.

When selling tomatoes, set aside the tomatoes that people do not want and sell them as canners. The leftover canners can become value-added products such as salsa, sauce, and soups. Alternatively, they become pig or chicken food. The goal is not to waste anything.

Personal note: We raise 4,000 tomato plants, which produce around 100,000 pounds of tomatoes. Now, I did not grow that many my first year, and it took some time to work our way to that number. However, we sell virtually every tomato. Our best market is two hours away, and we always sell out of tomatoes there. We have a few wholesale buyers, and a few roadside stands we service just because we want to make sure we have customers before and after the farmer's market season.

Production and growing

- **Soil and pH** - Tomatoes like soil with lots of organic material that is slightly acidic. The optimal pH is 6.0 to 7.0.
- **Nutrients** - Tomatoes need nitrogen (N) and calcium (Ca); for best results, use a 10-10-10 type fertilizer or the organic equivalent if growing organically.
- **Water** - Tomatoes need a steady supply of water. Too much water at once will cause cracks, and too little water will produce wilted and small fruit. For best results, deep-water a few times a week and use plastic mulch to help control water. Water at the bottom with a drip irrigation an inch or so from the stem to encourage root growth. Tomatoes require 1 to 2 inches of water a week, depending on temperature.
- **Spacing** - Tomatoes need spacing 24 to 26 inches in all directions. They need ample room to grow, so they are not competing for nutrients.
- **Growing Temp** - Tomatoes do not tolerate frost. They do best when the temperatures are between 65 to 95 degrees. If nighttime temperatures are above 85 degrees, fruits will not change color on the vine.
- **Pests** - Just about every pest likes tomatoes. The tomato hornworm is the most problematic. These are huge, green caterpillar-looking creatures with a fake stinger who feed on the stem. Flea beetles, aphids, and whiteflies are other troublesome tomato pests.

- **Disease** - Fusarium wilt typically shows up when plants are mature. Blossom End Rot occurs when ripening fruits develop a dark spot towards the bottom of the fruit. Other tomato diseases include blight, mosaic virus, and sunscald.
- **Hardiness Zones** - Tomatoes grow in all USDA zones.
- **Tips** - To for a steady harvest, stagger planting every few weeks. The second planting should be clones of the best plants from the first planting. Pick tomatoes as soon as they show the first sign of the desired color. When packing, place them top-down. Do not use refrigeration to store tomatoes. It will slow down the natural ripening process affecting the taste. Staking, caging, or stringing up increases yield and makes harvesting more efficient.
- **Harvest –** It is best to leave the tomatoes on the vine as long as possible. Harvest tomatoes when they reach the desired color. If the market day is a few days away, pick tomatoes slightly green to prevent them from over-ripening. Tomatoes should be firm when picked.

Companion Plants

Tomatoes play well with borage, marigolds, amaranth, basil, and garlic. Borage is a starflower that attracts pollinators while repelling tomatoes from hornworms. Marigolds repel pests, including root-knot nematodes. Amaranth and basil both repel insects and disease while improving tomato growth and flavor. Garlic is great to grow with tomatoes as it can reduce late blight.

Tomatoes do not get along with members of the cabbage family. Cabbages of all types will stunt tomato plant growth and reduce yields. Corn is problematic for tomato plants because the corn earworm likes tomatoes.

Mature dill plants will compete with tomatoes for nutrients and micronutrients, slowing tomato production. Also, avoid other nightshade plants such as eggplant, peppers, and potatoes because they are susceptible to early and late blight.

Uses

Tomatoes are a standalone food. Tomatoes find their way into salads and sandwiches. Tomatoes serve as the vital ingredient for ketchup, salsa, sauce, and chili. Tomatoes are sumptuous when grilling, boiling, basting, baking, and roasting.

Tomatoes provide an option for growers to tap into the farm-to-table movement. Tomatoes are the basis for many value-added products such as salsa, ketchup, pasta sauce, or other tomato-based items.

Tomatoes are high in lycopene, and as a result, many medical uses include preventing cancers, reducing heart disease, helping with cataracts and asthma. Tomatoes improve skincare when mixed with aloe-vera.

Fun Facts

- Tomatoes are indeterminate or determinate. Indeterminate vines grow until frost. Determinate tomatoes will stop growing once they reach a specific size.
- During the 1600s, people believed tomatoes to be bewitched and were called poison apple or witches' apple.
- Wild tomatoes grow in the Andes.
- A single serving of tomato provides 20 percent of daily vitamin requirements.
- Tomatoes are a great source of calcium.
- Tomatoes have high acidic content making them perfect canners.
- The U.S. Supreme Court ruled that tomatoes were to be legally treated as vegetables.
- Tomatoes are the state vegetable of New Jersey.
- Tomatoes are the official state fruit of Ohio, and tomato juice is the official beverage of Ohio.
- China is the largest producer of tomatoes.
- Tomatoes come in various colors, including green, yellow, orange, pink, black, brown, white, and purple.

- There are more than 7,500 tomato varieties grown around the world.
- Tomatoes are packed with calcium and potassium.
- Tomatoes are standard in Mediterranean cuisines.
- La Tomatina, the biggest tomato fight in the world, happens each year in the Spanish town of Buñol.
- At the Epcot Science Project at Walt Disney World, a single tomato plant produced 32,194 tomatoes.
- The heaviest tomato weighed in at 7 pounds 12 ounces.
- Tomatoes increase in weight as they ripen, even after harvesting.
- People consume 20 pounds of fresh tomatoes per year.
- As part of the *Tomatosphere* experiment, 600,000 tomato seeds traveled to the International Space Station before being planted in Canadian classrooms.

Selected Varieties

1884 Tomato is an indeterminate heirloom from Ohio. This heirloom produces large 1 to 2 pound pink or purple beefsteak style tomatoes. It is a very dynamic tomato with a timeless taste. This tomato has a loyal following in America's north-central region.

Amish Paste is an indeterminate heirloom tomato from the Amish community. Originating in Lancaster, this tomato follows the Amish community as it moves and expands. This oblong with an oxheart shape tomato is excellent for sauce making, slicing, and raw. This 8-ounce fruit sells well in all markets.

Ananas Noire Tomato is an indeterminate heirloom from France whose name is French for black pineapple. The Ananas Noire tomato is a successor of the Pineapple tomato. This tomato produces a dark purple, almost black fruit with pink streaks that weighs up to 1 ½ pounds. The flavor matches its beautiful exterior. A sweet, rich, and delicious tomato that creates repeat customers. This tomato grows into a giant plant that has heavy yields.

Azoychka Tomato is an indeterminate heirloom from Russia. It is a small, yellow beefsteak tomato that matures early, getting a tomato to market faster. This lemon-yellow fruit weighs a half-pound and is very flavorful with a slight citrus taste—an excellent option for salsa, salads, or sandwiches.

Black Krim Tomato is an indeterminate heirloom from the Black Sea region of Russia. This tomato weighs 3/4 lb. with a slightly salty taste. A good choice for people who like tomatoes and salt but want to limit their salt intake. The hotter the temperature, the darker the color of this tomato. This tomato performs better than most other tomatoes in the heat, and it routinely produces high yields.

Black Beauty Tomato is in an indeterminate heirloom from Russia with more antioxidants than any other tomato. It is the world's darkest tomato. It is an unlisted superfood that matches blueberries in nutrients but has a classic tomato taste with subtle earthy tones. This tomato has great storability, and it travels well. It takes longer to grow than other varieties.

Black Plum Tomato is an indeterminate heirloom from Russia with an elongated egg shape and looks like a Roma tomato with a fruity sweet taste. It is an excellent choice for snacking or adding to salads. These plants will produce a steady supply of tomatoes until frost.

Brandywine Tomato is an indeterminate heirloom from the Amish community famous for its rich and succulent flavor. It is a large pink tomato that grows up to 1 ½ pounds with creamy flesh. This tomato has been popular since its introduction in 1885 – a good seller that enhances the bottom line.

Bulgarian Triumph is an indeterminate heirloom from Bulgaria. This plant produces small, 2 to 4 ounce bright red tomatoes that grow in clusters. Unlike supermarket tomatoes, this tomato is intensely sweet and delectable. Customers must be allowed to sample this one so they fully grasp its superior taste and texture. The Bulgarian Triumph is a vigorous and productive tomato providing huge yields until frost.

Cherokee Purple Tomato is an indeterminate heirloom from Tennessee. It is one of the most sought-after tomatoes at most farmers markets. The highly productive plants produce a classic-looking tomato with a rose color that blends purple with deep red meat. This tomato is typically sliced and is the main ingredient for BLTs and tomato sandwiches.

It is one of the more difficult tomatoes to grow, and the thin skin and soft flesh make it challenging to transport. However, growers routinely report selling out and needing more of this faithful fruit.

Druzba Tomato is an indeterminate heirloom from Bulgaria. This tomato produces large, round, smooth fruit with a deep red that weighs up to a half-pound. This well-balanced tomato has just the right mix of sweetness, tartness, and juice. It is perfect for Hungarian goulash or other eastern European cuisines.

German Giant is an indeterminate heirloom from Germany. This massive, deep pink tomato weighs over 2 pounds. Its leaves look like potato leaves but on a vine. It has a rich taste, and it matures quickly. It is a dependable producer and is one of the easier heirlooms to grow.

Goldie Tomato is an indeterminate heirloom from Ohio. This tomato descended from the Giant Belgium, also from Ohio. The Goldie is a yellow tomato that has grown for over 150 years. This flavorful tomato grows on a vigorous vine and can easily weigh over two pounds. It is a great option to bring color to the market.

Gregori's Altai Tomato is an indeterminate heirloom from the Siberian and Chinese border in the Altai Mountains. This pink tomato weighs nearly a pound when mature. The Gregori's Altai is unique in that it is both sweet and acidic, giving it a more complex taste than other tomatoes. This tall plant produces heavy yields until frost. It is a good choice for Asian-influenced markets.

Hillbilly Tomato is an indeterminate heirloom from West Virginia that produces giant bi-colored yellowish-orange fruits with red streaks. Hillbilly tomatoes are sweet tasting with low acid weighing up to 2 pounds. This slicing tomato looks excellent when accompanied by red or purple tomatoes.

Indian Stripe Tomato is an indeterminate heirloom from Arkansas. This purple variety produces irregularly shaped fruit that weighs up to ¾ of a pound. It has a complex taste and is best when vine-ripened. It is similar to the Cherokee Purple, but it is easier to grow, bigger, and transports better. This plant is more compact than other varieties allowing more plants per row.

Lillian's Yellow Tomato is an indeterminate heirloom from Tennessee. This tomato is a large yellow tomato with low acid and a rich, complex, sweet flavor. This good slicer does great when grilled with a slice of cheese melted on it. The Lilian yellow is a meaty tomato with few seeds. It is one of the best producing, tasting, and most popular yellow tomatoes.

Mammoth German Gold Tomato is an indeterminate heirloom from Germany with fruits weighing two pounds. It has a deep gold color with red streaks. Its high sugar and acid make it an excellent canner and a good sauce option. This variety is from the 1800s and a perfect choice for growers that want to bring something unique to the market.

Marizol Purple Tomato is an indeterminate heirloom from Germany's Black Forest. It produces large, smooth, dark pink fruit with a purple tint and sweet flavor that weigh a pound—a very productive plant producing a consistent supply of tomatoes until frost.

Mortgage Lifter Tomato is an indeterminate heirloom from West Virginia. The profit from this tomato paid off the original grower's farm just before foreclosure. It is a substantial pink tomato with high demand. It has a few seeds and is very meaty with a classic form.

New Big Dwarf is a determinate heirloom introduced by the Isabella Seed Company in the early 1900s. This small plant only grows about 2 feet tall. This little plant produces large one-pound fruits. It is an excellent variety to sell as a plant or container plant in the spring. It has good yields for its size.

Principle Borghese Tomato is a determinate heirloom from the Tuscany region of Italy. It dries wells; this is an outstanding option for growers wanting to sell dried tomatoes as a value-added product. The Principle Borghese is a plum-shaped red tomato that has very little juice and just a few seeds. These plants are small but highly productive. This heirloom does not require staking.

Rutgers Tomato is a determinate heirloom from Rutgers University. It was the most popular tomato before mechanized harvesting and long-distance tomato transportation. Growers and customers consistently rank this as one of the best-tasting tomatoes and rave about its productivity. It is one of the more disease and cracking-resistant heirlooms.

Sausage Tomato is an indeterminate heirloom from unknown origins in Central America that grows 6 inches long and looks like a red banana pepper or sausage link. The Sausage tomato is a pasta-making or canning tomato. It is a very unusual and eye-catching tomato that is quite productive.

Stupice Tomato is an indeterminate heirloom from Czechoslovakia. It is one of the most cold-tolerant tomato plants; it can survive a light frost. It produces small, 2-ounce, low acid, sweet tomatoes. A quick to mature tomato that is highly productive and will bear fruit all season.

Tommy Toe Tomato is an indeterminate heirloom from Australia. A bright, elongated cherry-style tomato that is very prolific. A great-tasting full flavor tomato perfect for juicing. The Tommy Toe is very easy to grow a tomato. An excellent choice for new growers who want initial success.

Wild Cherry Tomato is an indeterminate heirloom from Mexico. It is a tiny tomato that grows wild, producing fruit only a half-inch in diameter, but this small fruit is full of flavor. This tomato is excellent for snacking or in salads — an easy to grow variety that practically grows itself.

Zigan Tomato is an indeterminate heirloom from Russia. This attractive, dark purple, almost black tomato has smooth skin with green shoulders. A great display item that customers love for the flavor. It is very rich in antioxidants making it healthier than other varieties. It is rare outside of Russia. Pick this tomato green and let it ripen off the vine for the best flavor.

Watermelons

"Watermelon is the chief of this world's luxuries, king by the grace of God over all the fruits of the earth. When one has tasted it, he knows what the angels eat. It was not a Southern watermelon that Eve took; we know it because she repented."
~ *Pudd'n Head Wilson*

Watermelon brings back memories of a simpler, enjoyable, and nostalgic time. Watermelons evoke images of sitting on a porch as generations connect. Watermelons provide food for communion as grandparents pass on family traditions to their grandchildren.

Watermelon is a lesson in patience, persistence, and purpose. Growing watermelon is 90 days of anticipation from planting the seed to harvest. Harvesting a watermelon is a race to the zenith of summertime activity. Watermelon is the common denominator that unites all summertime activities and condenses it into bite-sized pieces of heaven. Watermelons are summer.

History

Watermelons originated almost 5,000 years ago in the Kalahari Desert. From humble beginnings, watermelons meandered their way to Egypt. In Egypt, watermelons found a home. Here watermelons earned their place in society among the pharaohs. Pyramid hieroglyphics recorded watermelons, and watermelons joined kings as source water and nourishment for the afterlife.

In the beginning, watermelons were a water source. Through years of selective breeding, watermelons became the juicy and sweet fruit we know today. This sugary version of watermelon is what the Roman conquerors and merchants brought out of Egypt.

The Romans spread watermelons throughout their conquered lands in Europe. Eventually, watermelons made their way to the New World via slave ships. The first documented North American watermelon was in 1629 in Massachusetts.

Watermelons are a popular fruit in the Southern states, where they are also a profitable commercial crop. As the railroad developed and produce became easily transported, watermelon growers used transportability as their primary seed selection criteria. Watermelons are an essential part of Southern culture, and there are many watermelon-themed festivals throughout the south.

Competitive Advantage

Watermelons are summer's fruit. A cool melon tastes like summer and is always a treat. Many types of heirloom watermelons would be great sellers if someone paid attention to them. Watermelons are great to sell at farmers markets or roadside stands.

According to the USDA, watermelon growers grossed approximately $4,300 per acre in 2014. It does vary considerably among states and between seeded, seedless, and organic varieties. Some southern growers report making up to $8,000 or more per acre. Georgia growers can average as much as 50,000 pounds per acre, and at .20 per pound, that would be $10,000.00 per acre, and assuming full retail of .50 per pound, that would be $25,000.00!

Last year, 52% of people surveyed reported purchasing a watermelon in the past year. For the past few years, watermelon sales have increased 6% on average. Watermelons have a great price point for consumers and growers. They provide value to customers because they are big and provide value to growers because they increase average sale amounts.

The key to moving melons is to focus on varieties that have visual and taste appeal. Most melons in the retail market do not necessarily taste great. Retail melons concentrate on shipping and longer shelf life, and in many cases, they are picked just before their peak. *Local growers are at an advantage because they can focus on better-tasting varieties with more attractive looks.*

Marketing and Sales Strategies

Watermelons sell themselves in the summer. The most significant issue is keeping enough supply to meet demand. Offer fresh-cut options for those who do not want a whole watermelon or want to avoid a mess.

Watermelons are great sellers from the middle of June to the end of August. Having watermelons ready by the Fourth of July is a goal of most growers. In northern areas, this is difficult but doable with the use of hoop houses.

Watermelons are a great source of vitamins A and C. The red color comes from lycopene, a carotenoid pigment that helps fight cancer and other diseases.

There are many watermelon-based festivals and events. Local governments, farmer markets, and non-profits sponsor many. *To maximize sales, growers should consider hosting a watermelon festival or series of events.* Watermelon-themed events are great ways to tap into the growing farm-to-table movement and sell an experience.

Production and growing

- **Soil and pH** - Melons grow well in sandy loam soil with high organic matter such as composted manure. The optimum pH for melons is 6.0 to 6.5.
- **Nutrients** - Nitrogen (N) fuels high yields. By boosting leaf growth, nitrogen (N) also helps sugar accumulation in the fruit. Phosphorus (P) is required from flowering through to final fruit-fill to ensure good fruit set and fruit growth. Potassium (K) and calcium (Ca) are essential ingredients for cell and rind growth.
- **Water** - Melons require 1 to 2 inches of water every 7 to 10 days. Too much water at once will cause them to burst.

- **Spacing** – Plant watermelons 6 to 8 feet apart in all directions.
- **Growing Temp** - Melon seeds germinate between 70 and 90 degrees F.
- **Pests** - Insect pests are usually most critical in the seedling or early growth stage. Cucumber beetles, squash bugs, mites, and aphids are the most common insect pests of melons.
- **Disease** - Some foliar diseases appear when there is a reduction of air circulation. Foliar diseases appear first on leaves closest to the base of the main stem. Root diseases tend to occur where soil remains wettest, such as in low or high clay content areas.
- **Hardiness Zones** - Watermelon grows in USDA zones 3 - 11, with southern states being the best performer.
- **Tips** - When the seedlings have 1 or 2 true leaves, remove all but 2 or 3 healthy, well-spaced plants per hill. Watermelons grow best in manure compost.
- **Harvest** – Harvesting melons is tricky. People look for a dry tendril, or they thump it. The surest sign of ripeness in most watermelon varieties is the bottom spot's color, where the melon sits on the ground. As the watermelon matures, the area turns from almost white to a rich yellow. All watermelons lose the powdery or slick appearance on the top and take a dull look when fully ripe. It is one area where experience can be helpful, but do not let this deter you!

Companion Plants

Plant marigolds with melons. Marigolds will stimulate growth while deterring bean beetles, aphids, potato bugs, squash bugs, nematodes, and maggots, all of which will want to snack on melons.

Corn is another good companion plant. Once melons are established, the vines will choke out or smother weeds that would want to compete with corn. Okra is another great companion plant for the same reason. Typically, most tall plants do well with melons.

Lettuce and radishes, while low growing, tend to do well with melons. Lettuce and radish harvest is simultaneous with melon planting. It allows for better use of space. These early crops look great and suppress weed growth making the melon patch easier to work.

Melons and potatoes do not grow well together. Potatoes are ready for harvest just as the melons start to grow and bear fruit. Potato harvesting requires digging, and there is no safe way to dig potatoes out of a melon patch. Also, potato plants are at their peak height when it is time to plant melons. It creates a sunblock, and melons require full sun. Potatoes are attractive to many melon-loving pests. Having these two plants together increases the risk of blight that can destroy both crops.

Uses

Watermelons are an excellent beta-carotene source, folic acid, potassium, vitamin C, and dietary fiber. Watermelons are a superfood that reduces cholesterol, lowers stress, and aids in weight management. Watermelons are a significant weapon in the fight against cancer.

Watermelons are a great source of vitamin B. A diet high in vitamin B allows people to more efficiently process sugars and carbs, especially harmful processed carbs. It provides the dual benefit of weight control and extra energy. One of the fantastic benefits of watermelons is that it contains collagen.

The most common use of watermelons is as food. Watermelons are great by themselves, as part of fruit salad, or as a garnish. Also, melons are perfect for juices and drink making. They also make impressive displays when cut in interesting ways or when hollowed out and used as a fruit basket.

Watermelons are perfect for breakfast, lunch, dinner, or snacks. Watermelon cocktails are also fun and delicious. Watermelons based drinks (both alcoholic and non-alcoholic) are fun when cooking out during the hot days of summer.

Fun Facts

- In a Vietnamese folklore, watermelon symbolizes luck and goes by the name *dua hau*.

- The ancient Egyptians used wild watermelons as a water source.
- The ancient Greek name for watermelon was *pepon*.
- The explorers used watermelons as canteens.
- There are more than 1,200 varieties of watermelon.
- Florida leads the nation in watermelon production.
- In China, watermelon rinds are stir-fried or stewed.
- In the South, watermelon rinds are pickled.
- The largest recorded watermelon was 350.5 pounds.
- The watermelon is the state vegetable of Oklahoma.
- During the Civil War, the Confederate Army boiled watermelon to make molasses for cooking.
- Scientists created cube-shaped melons.
- By weight, watermelon is the most-consumed fruit in the U.S.
- Watermelons were a political protest symbol for Palestinians.
- Watermelon seeds are a great source of protein.

Selected Varieties

Ali Baba Watermelon is a red meated heirloom from Iraq that has excellent flavor. Its thick rind makes it a good shipper. The Ali Baba adapts well to most conditions and is easy to grow. The Ali Baba is a light green, oblong watermelon that weighs between 15 to 30 pounds.

Arikara Watermelon is a small pink meated heirloom from North Dakota. This watermelon is a descendant of the Spanish watermelon developed by the Arikara tribe and is a first-class personal watermelon with dark rinds. The Arikara is a sweet melon that dates back to the 1800s. This watermelon's Native American history makes a great marketing story.

Black Diamond Watermelon is a red meated heirloom from Arkansas, also called the Arkansas Black Diamond. It was developed in Hope, Arkansas, not far from the Murfreesboro diamond mine. The Black Diamond watermelon grows to 40 pounds. This mid-season melon ripens at the peak of summer; it is a tough-skinned melon with large leaves to prevent sunburn. It is a very drought tolerant variety.

Black Spanish Watermelon is a red meated heirloom from Spain. The Moors brought this watermelon to Philadelphia in the early 1880s. This melon's fruits are squatted and oblong, with deep ribbing and a thick blackish-green rind. This thick rind makes this a suitable choice for shipping and taking to market.

Cuban Queen Watermelon is a red meated heirloom from the 1800s. An early producer, this melon has a sweet, crisp flesh. This easy-to-grow melon does well in difficult areas. The Cuban Queen grows to be 35 pounds.

Cream of Saskatchewan is a white meated heirloom from Russia. This watermelon grows well in New England and other northern areas. It is small, weighing under 10 pounds; it is a perfect icebox melon that is crisp and sweet. The Cream of Saskatchewan is unique and attention-getting.

Desert King Watermelon is a yellow meated watermelon that ripens mid-season. This 20-pound melon has light green skin and beautiful yellow flesh. This Arkansas favorite grows well throughout the south, is always a great seller, and is a good choice for drought-prone areas.

Dixie Queen Watermelon is a classic pink meated heirloom from the south. This large round melon grows up to 30 pounds with a crisp and sweet inside. This light green melon sports the classic dark green watermelon stripes. The Dixie Queen rind is thin but stout.

This watermelon dates back to the late 1880s and consistently rates as one of the best growers. This melon's name is a good choice for growers looking for a festival name – think of the "Salem Dixie Queen Festival" or "Ozark Family Farm Dixie Queen Melon Festival."

Georgia Rattlesnake is a red meated heirloom from Georgia. This deep-rooted variety dates back to the mid-1880s. The Georgia Rattlesnake is a very productive melon producing long fruits weighing 30 pounds. The exterior of this watermelon is light green with dark green irregular stripes. It is a good watermelon for any farmer's markets or roadside stands.

Ice Cream Watermelon is a medium-sized pink flesh heirloom from the 1880s that gets its name from being as sweet as ice cream. It is a clever choice for growers looking for something with a fascinating history. This thin-skinned melon does not travel long distances well, but it can make a short trip to local markets or roadside stands.

King and Queen Watermelon is a pink flesh heirloom with light green skin. This watermelon is a winter melon and will store well into November. This watermelon is not as sweet as other melons, but it does have more lycopene, which increases its marketability. The King and Queen travel well and weigh around 9 pounds. It is a popular fruity with the Midwestern Mennonites who pickle this watermelon.

Kleckley's Sweet Watermelon is a red meated heirloom from the 1800s in Georgia. This watermelon is scarce in retail stores because the thin skin makes it difficult to transport. The Kleckley is an oblong, dark green watermelon that grows up to 40 pounds. This watermelon is sweeter than most other varieties with a larger heart. Kleckley creates repeat customers.

Klondike Blue Ribbon Striped Watermelon is a bright red meated heirloom from California. Its popularity started around 1900 when it began winning blue ribbons around California. From there, it spread across the nation. It has thin but tough skin allowing it to be transported short distances. It produces intensely sweet fruits that weigh up to 11 pounds. This variety is great for cookouts, BBQs, or picnics with its classic homegrown taste.

Mabry's Yellow Watermelon is a yellow meated heirloom from Georgia. This large, round solid dark green (almost black) watermelon weighs up to 40 pounds; it's a great-tasting and juicy fruit that builds customer loyalty. Mabry dates back to the early 1900s. It is an easy-to-grow melon that can withstand weather changes.

Moon and Stars Watermelon is a yellow meated or sometimes pink meated watermelon from Rocky Ford, Colorado. The dark green skin of the fruit has yellow dots resembling the nighttime sky. The thick rinds are good for pickling. The Moon and Stars leaves are light green with yellow speckles.

Mountain Sweet Watermelon is a deep yellow meated heirloom first grown at Jefferson's Monticello. This watermelon produces fruits that weigh 20 - 35 pounds. This high sugar melon dates back to the 1840s when it was trendy in the Northeast.

Orange Flesh Tendersweet Watermelon is an orange/yellow meated heirloom. This watermelon has high sugar content. The fruit of this melon is oblong and weighs up to 45 pounds. The rinds are light green, medium-thick, and suitable for pickling.

Sweet Siberian Watermelon is a yellow meated heirloom from Russia. This watermelon is medium-sized and weighs 10 pounds with a dark green rind. This melon is sweet and is appropriate for northern markets; it is a very productive watermelon with vigorous vines and many fruits.

Tom Watson Watermelon is a red meated heirloom from Georgia. This large 40-pound melon is named for a Georgian grower who commercialized it. Tom Watson has a thick rind and is a good shipper and pickling watermelon. One of the fastest-growing giant watermelons, this melon matures in just under 90 days.

Will's Sugar Watermelon is a red meated heirloom from South Dakota. It is a 12-pound melon with a forest green rind. It was developed in the 1880s, and its high sugar makes it great for commercial growers.

Made in the USA
Coppell, TX
05 February 2023

12199897R00194